# The Road to AI
## Mankind's Technological Journey

## Andy Boerger
### Kazuo Hanazaki   Miki Hanazaki

**KINSEIDO**

**Kinseido Publishing Co., Ltd.**
3-21 Kanda Jimbo-cho, Chiyoda-ku,
Tokyo 101-0051, Japan

Copyright © 2021 by Andy Boerger
                Kazuo Hanazaki
                Miki Hanazaki

First published 2021 by Kinseido Publishing Co., Ltd.

Cover design　Takayuki Minegishi

 音声ファイル無料ダウンロード

http://www.kinsei-do.co.jp/download/4124

この教科書で  DL 00 の表示がある箇所の音声は、上記 URL または QR コードにて無料でダウンロードできます。自習用音声としてご活用ください。

▶ PC からのダウンロードをお勧めします。スマートフォンなどでダウンロードされる場合は、**ダウンロード前に「解凍アプリ」をインストール**してください。
▶ URL は、**検索ボックスではなくアドレスバー(URL 表示欄)**に入力してください。
▶ お使いのネットワーク環境によっては、ダウンロードできない場合があります。

🔘 CD 00 　左記の表示がある箇所の音声は、教室用 CD (Class Audio CD) に収録されています。

# Preface

I wrote this book because I feel that as we move forward, it sometimes helps to step back—to take in the larger picture. Today, technology advances so rapidly that conjecture about a near future where computers move far beyond humans in intelligence is no longer science fiction. Many now take it as a given that within our lifetimes a "Singularity" will occur, after which the destiny of planet Earth (and some boldly predict, the entire universe!) will belong to the machines that we are busily creating today. We will pass the baton to our creation, in other words.

Predictions (and warnings) about technology overtaking humans go back at least as far as Mary Shelley's *Frankenstein*, which was published two centuries ago. However, today—with machine learning, Big Data, the "cloud," etc.—they have begun to appear more plausible.

But how concerned should we be? After all, technology has *always* played an immensely transformative role in society. In fact, there has never been a truly revolutionary technological breakthrough that didn't change not only our culture and our physical surroundings, but also the way humans think. Agriculture, architecture, the printing press, the automobile, mass media, etc.; all have had an enormous impact. Will AI be uniquely *more* revolutionary, or is it just the next destination along a long, long journey?

That is the question that this book considers, without attempting a clear-cut answer. A few decades from now, we will have our answer. Either AI will have taken over, and robots far more intelligent than Einstein will be everywhere, or humans will still be the dominant intelligence on the planet, using AI to transform our world (as we have already begun to do), while re-maining in charge of it.

*Until* we know, we will have to keep pondering, and guess-ing. That makes this era—the dawn of The Age of AI—mysterious and exciting, as well as a bit scary! Mostly, I feel it is uncertainty about just how far AI will go that makes us uneasy about it. I began teaching a course at Yokohama National University to help my students form clear-headed ideas about AI by placing it in its proper historical context, alongside other breakthrough tech-nologies. I approached Kinseido with the proposal to turn that course into a textbook, and they kindly consented. This book, and the overview of technology spanning millennia that it provides, is meant to help students make educated guesses about where we are headed.

Andy Boerger

# Contents

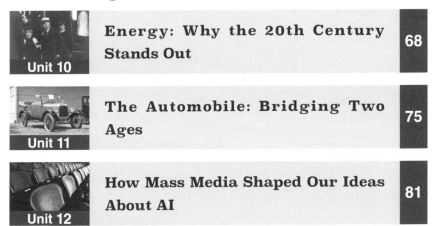
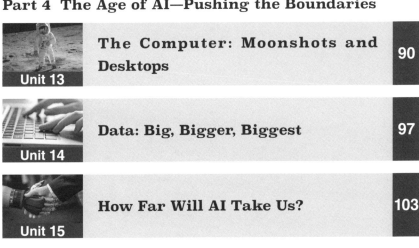

# Part 1

## The Age of Tools
### —The Early Part
### of the Journey

# Unit 1

## Introduction: How Far Can Tech Take Us?

🎧 DL 002 ~ 013   ⊙ CD1-02 ~ ⊙ CD1-13

Picture this everyday scene: you are riding a commuter train in a big city, while, across from you, a

5  mother plays peek-a-boo with her baby. If asked to guess, just how old do you think that

happy infant will grow up to be? Eighty? One hundred? Stretch your imagination a bit. How about three hundred? A thousand?

Or more? Even much, much more?

If a passenger seated next to you were to predict, with a straight face, that the infant would live *forever*, what would your reaction be? Just to be clear, there is nothing at all unusual about this particular baby. The person making the astounding predic- 5 tion is merely using this one baby as an example. He believes that nearly every infant alive today has the same probability of achieving immortality!

In any other era, you would conclude that the person is delusional, but not in this era. For we live in an age when techno- 10 logical advances are taking place so rapidly that there are indeed educated, rational people arguing that babies born today have a good chance of living forever.

Just how does a newborn baby get from what we commonly think of as a normal human lifespan to eternal life? Simply 15 by following the current trajectory of scientific innovations and discoveries. Lifespans are increasing day by day, due to advancements in medicine, and breakthroughs in understanding the human genome. Scientists all over the world are working hard to "crack the code" of human biology and understand the aging 20 process so that eventually we can treat it like any other illness or disease. It is not unusual, even today, for people to live beyond one hundred (very rare in previous centuries), with Japan being the leader in this new world of centenarians.

Think forward to the next one hundred years that babies 25 born today can reasonably be expected to live through, and compare it to the last one hundred years. Is it not truly astounding just how much progress the human race has achieved in the most recent century? An everyday item that we take for granted, such as a smartphone or a car's GPS system, would have been consid- 30 ered impossible a hundred years ago.

Human beings a century ago were busy familiarizing themselves with a new invention—the telephone—that made it possible to speak with someone thousands of kilometers away, and another—the automobile—that made it possible to travel across a continent in a matter of days, rather than months or years. Along they came, one after the other, these miraculous inventions of the 20th century: telephones, automobiles, radios, refrigerators, televisions, airplanes, computers. Not to mention the number of diseases that were cured or eradicated in the same time period. That was one very eventful century!

Continuing along the same trajectory, it is easy to see where the idea of people living forever comes from. If someone born today lives until the year 2120, imagine the incredible technology they will be surrounded by. Is it outlandish to think that some time within the following hundred years, miracles of technology will appear that will actually make death obsolete?

That brings us to Artificial Intelligence (AI). Some have already referred to it as humanity's "final invention," because once it surpasses human intelligence, all further important inventions and innovations will come not from human beings, but from the superior intelligence we will create.

Predictions about AI range from the miraculous—it will enable humans to live happily forever, never needing to work or suffer again—to nightmarish—it will enslave us and consider us as little more than cockroaches to be controlled, suppressed or even destroyed. Although both scenarios, the utopian and the dystopian, are currently limited to science fiction novels and movies, they may not be for much longer. Futurists have posited a "Singularity" event (the exact point when computers overtake humans in all forms of intelligence and then rapidly move beyond us) occurring as soon as 2045, very much within our lifetimes.

We are sure to read and learn more about AI with each passing year, as we close in on the hypothetical "Singularity" and all the changes it may bring.

On the other hand, could it be that all this talk about super-human intelligence, a "Singularity," and immortal babies is just a lot of hype? Science fiction rather than science fact? In order to make reasonable guesses about where AI will take us, it is helpful to take a historical perspective. After all, AI is the latest invention in a long history of technological advances that have transformed the human race, and not always for the better.

As we move through the units of this book, we will travel back to mankind's earliest technological achievements, and re-trace our steps along the "Road to AI" that we have traveled over millennia. In doing so, it is my hope that we will achieve a clear perspective. We may be able to see AI less as a singular transfor-mative event, and more as a logical progression of technological developments and inventions that have been transforming us all along. In other words, in order to get a better sense of where we are going, let's take a tour of where we have been, and how far we have come. Once upon a time…

# Exercises

**A** Choose the definition of the words as they are used in the essay.

1. delusional
2. outlandish
3. obsolete
4. hypothetical
5. hype

a. something that is being greatly exaggerated
b. based on an idea or theory
c. very odd or ridiculous
d. persuaded of things that are illogical or impossible
e. outdated and belonging to an earlier era

**B** Choose the correct answer to complete each sentence.

1. Regarding human immortality, the author appears to say
   a. that it is an idea that no one should actually take seriously.
   b. that it is an interesting proposition, but should not be simply assumed at this point.
   c. that it is a certainty at some point, based on the rate of technological advances.

2. The author compares 20th century technology to future technology
   a. to imply that future technology will achieve far superior results.
   b. to suggest that we will be no more ready for it than people were for the telephone and the automobile.
   c. to provide useful context to assess predictions about what might be achieved in the future.

3. The author of the passage would definitely agree that

   **a.** an AI "Singularity" event will certainly appear in our life-times.

   **b.** AI is an important technology that will have profound influence on society.

   **c.** AI will either be very positive or very negative, not something in between.

## C Discuss the topics.

1. If technology moves fast enough that it makes it possible for you to live forever (or at least for thousands of years), would you want to? Why or why not? If you have children someday, would you want it for them? Why or why not?

2. If a "Singularity" occurs, and results in humans having inferior intelligence compared to AI, what role do you see for humans in such a future? Would you want to live in a world where mankind's inventions are smarter than mankind?

3. Based on what you know about how humans have used technology up to the present, do you think it is more likely that AI will lead to a positive and beneficial future, or a future that contains greater threats and harm? Give reasons for your answer.

# Unit 2

# Extending Both Muscle Power and Brainpower

DL 014 ~ 024   CD1-14 ~ CD1-24

Today, we have computer programs that can defeat any chess master, or *igo* (a more difficult game) master. In the near future, AI is predicted to greatly enhance the power of the human brain. By connecting our own brains to AI technology, we will be able to learn more quickly than any humans in history. Each of us in the future may become an "Einstein." This has parallels to how our ancestors deep in the past began to use *tools* to greatly enhance the power of the human body; the very beginning of our technological journey.

Long ago, we used tools to build stronger "bodies" for ourselves; bodies that could lift, carry, dig, hunt, etc., far more effectively than what was permitted by our own muscular limitations. *Manual tools*, the first technology, separated hominids from other species and showed that the natural world could be manipulated.  5

Some of the oldest tools displayed in the British Museum in London are arrowheads from around two million years ago. These were fashioned by *homo habilis*, ancestors of *homo sapiens* who dwelled in a region that is now part of Tanzania. With the emergence of *homo sapiens* (around 200,000 years ago) we find the shape of arrowheads and other simple stone tools being modified over time for specialized purposes. From very early on, *homo sapiens* was an innovator.  15

Homo habilis

10

As familiarity with tool use grew, so did familiarity with the "master tool" that ran all the others: the human brain. A positive feedback loop between man and tools jumpstarted our evolution and caused us to become, primarily, a technological species.

We used our brains to conceptualize what tools could be and  20
do. Moreover, the use of the tools refined our brain power. Just as small children develop their brains by playing with building blocks, early human tool use developed key regions in the brain related to higher thought, and planted the seeds of *reasoning* in us. Eventually we learned to think and plan *together*, in groups,  25
to achieve greater results than could be achieved individually, giving rise to civilization. Hunting tribes of *homo sapiens* grew from just a dozen or so members to eventually numbering in the hundreds. Tool use enabled us to develop a skill that has been part of every technological development since: *Organization*.  30

We can see organization emerging by looking at *agriculture*, considered the most important early technological development. Tool use began roughly two million years ago, but it was only about ten thousand years ago where we see the development of agriculture on a large scale. With agriculture, human beings found it necessary to *organize* at scales and in ways they had not done previously.

The earliest agricultural tools were stones used to scratch at the earth for planting seeds. These were tools already being used by hunter-gatherers to dig for roots and insects. As with arrowheads, these tools gradually grew more specialized. Hoes, plows, shovels, etc., were invented and refined into the specialized farming equipment that can be seen in ancient Egyptian artwork dating back thousands of years.

As our tools got better, so did our organizational skills. We organized topography, digging furrows and irrigation channels, and built storage spaces for seeds, etc. We organized time itself, planting and harvesting according to pre-planned schedules based on the seasons. Early farming communities organized space and time in more sophisticated ways than not only other species, but rival hunter-gatherer societies as well. Thus, our brains adjusted, learning to think more logically, plan more long-term, innovate and modify to increase yields, etc. In other words, the ways we use our brains today, in business, government, science, and education, were seeded in us by our agricultural lifestyle.

Similarly to agriculture, architecture also changed both our outer/geographical space and our inner/mental space. When food is a moving target, as it generally is for hunter-gatherers, domiciles tend to be temporary. They can either be broken down and reassembled elsewhere or simply abandoned. Animal skins (draped over branches) and straw were the most common early home materials, and continue to be today for the remaining hunter-gatherer tribes.

In early agricultural communities, tools not only for farming, but also for building became necessary, further stimulating our rapidly developing brains. In addition to the plows, shovels, etc., that were needed to farm, early humans developed bricks, hammers, nails, saws, etc., in order to erect structures that were durable and permanent (how permanent? Why, look at the Pyramids of Giza, still standing proudly six thousand years later!)

Pyramid of Giza

5

10

15

This was an exciting time in human history, when dozens of specialized tools were invented and improved upon in rapid succession across early agricultural settlements spanning the globe. All the while, the "master tool," the human brain, developed, separating itself from the brains of other species through the continual mental challenges that the technological lifestyle provided. Our partnership with technology had begun.

20

# Exercises

**A** Choose the definition of the words as they are used in the essay.

1. enhance      a. similarity
2. parallel      b. place where a person lives
3. manual      c. operated by hand
4. conceptualize      d. form an idea
5. domicile      e. improve the quality of

**B** Choose the correct answer to complete each sentence.

1. The author states that the use of tools by early man
   a. enabled them to defeat other animals.
   b. developed and refined the human brain.
   c. began with the emergence of *homo sapiens*.

2. According to the author, agriculture
   a. emerged very early in human history.
   b. challenged humans to increase their organizational capabilities.
   c. was rejected by most hunter-gatherer tribes.

3. Architecture developed as an outgrowth of agriculture because
   a. agricultural tools were also used to build homes.
   b. tents and thatched huts had to be abandoned in farming communities.
   c. agriculture made permanent settlements possible.

## C Discuss the topics.

1. The species *homo sapiens* has existed for more than 200,000 years, but agricultural communities have existed for only about 10,000 years. Why do you suppose it took such a long time for agriculture to appear?

2. Think of the tools that you use on a regular basis, either manual or digital (or a combination of the two); how are they different from early human tools, and how are they the same? Can you think of ways that the tools you use affect your thinking?

3. Many educators today fear that less exposure to manual tools in early education risks stunting a child's brain. Do you feel that children in today's technological society are not getting enough exposure to simple hand tools such as scissors, building blocks, etc.? If you were an educator, how would you address the situation?

# Unit 3

## Agriculture: A Mistake?

DL 025 ~ 036    CD1-25 ~ CD1-36

Mankind's relationship with technology can be likened to a marriage. It is a long-term partnership that has provided us with many of the things that an ideal marriage does, such as comfort, security and enjoyment. However, not all marriages are ideal.

5 Similarly, our relationship with technology has had moments that have caused us to question its overall benefit.

"I have become Shiva, Destroyer of Worlds." This line from the Bhagavad Gita was recalled by American physicist J. Robert Oppenheimer when he witnessed the first testing of the atomic

weapon that he had devoted so much of his
career to developing. The atomic bombs used
at the end of WWII revealed technology at its
most violent and destructive. Today, the threat
of nuclear weapons remains, but we can add to
that the rapid destruction of the environment
and climate change.

J. Robert Oppenheimer

Fears of nuclear warfare and catastroph-
ic climate change go back only about half a century. However,
historian/anthropologist Jared Diamond and others suggest that
mankind's "marriage" to technology was doomed from the start!
To these contrarian scholars, agriculture—widely regarded as the
most important early human technology—should be viewed not
as a triumph but rather as a tragedy; a mistake from which the
human race never managed to recover.

Agriculture a mistake? The idea runs counter to nearly everything we've been taught about it from childhood. Calling it a
mistake is a provocative argument designed to get us to rethink
our entire history more critically. So, what are the arguments,
and how seriously should we take them?

Let's begin with food. Is the food we eat today healthier than
what our ancestors in hunter-gatherer tribes ate? Diamond ar-
gues no. He points out that much of our modern, agricultural diet
comes from just a few grains, basically rice, wheat, and increasingly, corn. A lot of what we consume is empty calories that fill
the stomach but don't actually nourish the body. The price we pay
for that ranges from lethargy to obesity to heart disease.

Hunter-gatherers may have consumed fewer calories, but
they supplied their body with a wider range of sources of protein
and necessary minerals and vitamins from the many animal and

5

10

15

20

25

30

**Unit 3** Agriculture: A Mistake? 23

plant sources available to them, such as eggs and nuts. Indeed, that wider range included bugs! But bugs are an exceptional protein source that the body is much better equipped to digest than potato chips or candy bars.

5    In terms of lifestyles, hunter-gatherers lived much like other animals did (and the few remaining tribes do even today in remote areas of the world), fitting into their ecosystems rather than radically transforming them as agriculturalists do.

We may imagine such a lifestyle as very difficult, but if we
10   look at the remaining hunter-gatherer tribes today, it turns out they work *less*, not more, than we do. Members of such tribes are able to take those afternoon naps that modern office workers are either unable to take or made to feel guilty for taking. For further comparison, our closest animal relatives, gorillas and chimps,
15   get about a third more sleep than we do, indicating that perhaps that's what our own bodies prefer. Agriculture, by forcing a schedule of planting and harvesting upon people who practice it, created unnatural working and sleeping patterns that our bodies pay the price for.

20   So, by getting better food, more sleep, and being spared backbreaking work such as digging furrows and building grain storage facilities, it is not surprising to learn that our hunter-gatherer ancestors were actually healthier in important ways. They were taller, more fit, had better teeth, etc. It is true that
25   they lived considerably shorter lives, on average. But most of the progress we have made in terms of increasing longevity has only come about in the last 150 years. For most of our agrarian history, humans did not have longer lifespans than our hunter-gatherer ancestors.

30   There are other examples in history of skeptics questioning

our relationship with technology. An obvious one is the automobile, which is frequently
condemned by environmen-
talists. There is no doubt that
the invention of the automobile was an important turning

point for mankind. Not only in terms of transporting people and
goods, but also in terms of economics and employment, the car
industry's influence has been enormous. Nevertheless, we must
consider its downside. Air pollution chokes major cities (particularly in the developing world), and $CO_2$ emissions from hundreds
of millions of cars on the road have had disastrous effects on the
environment. If, in this century (as some scientists predict) the
"greenhouse effect" caused by fossil fuel emissions raises the
global temperature to the point at which it threatens our very
survival as a species, will we truly be able to argue that the benefits of cars have been worth it?

Then we come to AI. Many dystopian movies, novels, etc.,
depict conscious AI machines overtaking human intelligence, and
then either destroying or enslaving us. Again we see the same
fear of going too far with technology, using it recklessly, in foolish
and harmful ways that we later come to regret.

In spite of these concerns, technology marches forward. It is
like a genie we can't put back in its lamp once it's been released.
We cannot stop the progress of AI just as we cannot go back to
being hunter-gatherers, or un-invent the automobile. Our task,
therefore, is to make wise choices and use technology in ways
that do more good than harm.

# Exercises

**A** Choose the definition of the words as they are used in the essay.

1. liken
2. anthropologist
3. agrarian
4. choke
5. dystopian

a. describing a negative future
b. related to farming
c. compare
d. make difficult to breathe
e. person who studies human cultures

**B** Choose the correct answer to complete each sentence.

1. The author states that climate change
   a. has now become a bigger threat than nuclear war.
   b. seems likely to increase the possibility of nuclear war.
   c. is a threat to civilization on par with nuclear war.

2. Regarding agriculture and longevity,
   a. it erases all doubt that agriculture was a mistake.
   b. the connection may be less persuasive than people imagine.
   c. there is actually no connection between the two.

3. The fear that AI may eventually be considered a mistake
   a. is comparable to how the value of other technologies have been questioned.
   b. is less realistic than concerns about agriculture and the automobile.
   c. should be taken more seriously than concerns about agriculture and the automobile.

## C Discuss the topics.

1. The argument that agriculture was a mistake is shocking to most people, as well as unpersuasive. What arguments can you think of in support of agriculture?

2. Would you like to spend some time, such as a year, living with one of the remaining hunter-gatherer tribes, such as along the Amazon or in Papua New Guinea? Why or why not?

3. Most people believe that agriculture has benefitted humans greatly, but what about other animals? Can you think of any species other than humans that have benefitted from the human practice of agriculture? If not, do you think that should be included in the argument that agriculture was a mistake? Why or why not?

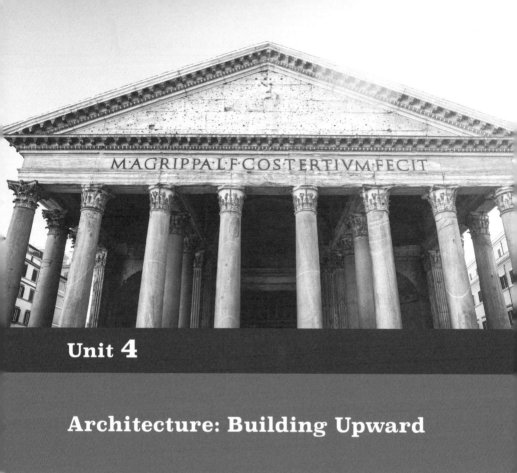

MAGRIPPA·L·F·COS·TERTIVM·FECIT

# Unit 4

# Architecture: Building Upward

DL 037 ~ 047    CD1-37 ~    CD1-47

A great deal has been written about the tremendous role
that agriculture played in forming human society. It laid such
foundations of civilization as division of labor and long term
planning. Let's now turn to another development that arose in
5    early human settlements: architecture. Let's consider how the art
of building upward has influenced the human species.

New York City's Chrysler Building is an iconic structure,
one of the most famous features of the legendary Manhattan
skyline. For a very brief time—a mere eleven months—it was the

world's tallest structure (318 meters), before the even more iconic Empire State Building (443 meters) overtook it.

Chrysler Building

However, the Chrysler Building can forever hold onto another significant distinction; 5 by besting the Eiffel Tower (300 meters), which it did in 1930, it was the first time in human history that the world's tallest structure was inhabitable, with elevators, lighting and toilet facilities, all the way up to the top! The building contains 77 stories of workers dili- 10 gently going about their daily duties higher than birds. By proudly sending people to the sky in the office buildings in Manhattan such as the Chrysler Building and the Empire State Building, mankind—perhaps even more than it had done with the invention of the airplane a few decades earlier—had made a home of 15 the sky.

Previous to the Chrysler Building, all the world's tallest structures had been temples, towers and cathedral spires, from the Great Pyramid at Giza four millennia ago to the Eiffel Tower. Unlike skyscrapers, they were inhabitable only in the lower 20 floors, while the upper portions of the structure served mostly symbolic purposes. For thousands of years, mankind has built upward, ever upward.

The technological innovations of architecture have resulted in expanding the dimensions of habitation. Hunter-gatherer 25 tribes primarily live two dimensionally, feet to earth. In contrast, many modern urban dwellers spend most of each day anywhere from five to five hundred meters above ground. Architecture enables humans to inhabit a three dimensional plane, having achieved the ability to overcome gravity, like wingless birds, us- 30

**Unit 4** Architecture: Building Upward 29

ing the power of our minds, rather than feathers, to move about high above the earth.

Agriculture, as we have seen, inserted Organization into humanity's cognitive toolbox. Architecture added another important feature to it: Structure. It is likely that the earliest agricultural peoples continued to dwell inside the same types of homes as their hunter-gatherer predecessors, but they needed something more permanent and weather-resistant to protect the grain they depended upon for survival. Keeping grain secure and dry presented a challenge that animal skin coverings or thatched grass could not adequately address. And so our ingenious early ancestors invented bricks, and architecture was born.

Bricks provided more protection from the elements than earlier construction materials. However, they came with their own dangers. Being heavier and denser than animal skins and thatched grass, bricks falling down on those beneath them resulted in serious injuries and even fatalities. Thus, the use of bricks (as well as stones) required our ancestors to solve problems via more complex thinking than even agriculture had required. Building upward—while making sure that the top didn't collapse down onto whatever was beneath it—raised the level of human cognition. In other words, our mental world was elevated, just as our physical world was. Humans needed to devise safe, sturdy structures.

From the ingenious design of pyramids—which enabled workers to build steadily upward with a solid footing upon successive tiers from which to work upon— to columns, vaults and suspension

Parthenon

pylons, early human architects continually innovated and improvised, resulting in ingenious and beautiful structures, such as the proud columns of the Parthenon of Athens and the impressive dome of the Pantheon in Rome that still stand today, thousands of years later. 5

Living in permanent settlements, people in farm communities gradually brought architecture into every element of their lives. Beginning with grain storage facilities, they moved on to walls to protect their village from invaders, thence to temples, onward to homes, schools, libraries, etc. Agricultural people's lives 10 revolved around architecture just as the lives of hunter-gatherers revolved around the natural world of forests and coastlines. Humans became preoccupied with structure, improving their building technologies to produce not only increasingly stable structures, but also ones that were increasingly aesthetically pleasing. 15 Far more than agriculture, architecture provided early man with the opportunity to develop his artistic side.

The challenge of building permanent structures transformed human thought, equal to the degree that agriculture had done. 20 Even today, the pairing of Agriculture and Architecture remains at

the heart of modern society. Cities—and the farms that sustain them—have maintained their importance as the foundation of a 25 functioning society for over ten thousand years. Organization and Structure have maintained their importance as foundational elements of every subsequent human innovation and development throughout history, from government to religion to banking to education to warfare, as well as the technological innovations that 30 have paved the Road to AI.

Who would have imagined, all that time ago, that the simple decision to stay in one place, growing food there and building dwellings for the long term could have so radically altered human evolution? Yet that is exactly what happened. With those two early developments, mankind began seeding the technological world we inhabit today.

## Exercises

**A** **Choose the definition of the words as they are used in the essay.**

| | |
|---|---|
| 1. iconic | **a.** important |
| 2. significant | **b.** extremely |
| 3. cognitive | **c.** focused on |
| 4. preoccupied | **d.** related to thinking |
| 5. radically | **e.** very famous or popular |

**B** **Choose the correct answer to complete each sentence.**

1. The author feels the Chrysler Building is important because
   **a.** for a brief time it was the world's tallest building.
   **b.** it was the first fully inhabitable building to be the world's tallest structure.
   **c.** it pioneered important engineering features such as elevators.

2. Bricks were a breakthrough development because they
   **a.** made it possible to store necessary grains for agriculture.
   **b.** eliminated the need for animal skins in building shelters.
   **c.** could be used to create stronger walls than were used by hunter-gatherer tribes.

3. Architecture modified human thinking because
   **a.** it was used to build schools and libraries.
   **b.** the necessity of building safe structures elevated human problem-solving.
   **c.** it introduced art and beauty into human culture.

**C** Discuss the topics.

1. Describe your ideal city. Is it filled with new, shiny skyscrapers or old historical ones (or a combination)? What is the ratio of buildings to natural grounds such as parks? Does it have plazas, fountains, etc.? How many people live there? Explain what makes this city ideal to you.

2. Architecture can be used to generate feelings of safety and contemplation. It can also generate feelings of excitement and surprise. How does architecture affect you in your daily life? How do the rooms you occupy affect your moods and thoughts?

3. According to the author, architecture introduced Structure to man's way of thinking. Today, we see structure in how we design our government, our education system, our businesses and companies, etc. Is it possible that we have placed too much emphasis on structure? If so, can you think of ways to allow for more freedom and spontaneity in society?

# Unit 5

# Building Better Brains: Technology and Thinking

DL 048 ~ 057   CD1-48 ~ CD1-57

We tend to take thinking for granted. We sit and quietly muse to ourselves, finding words in our heads to match the concepts floating around up there. Or we formulate a line of thought with which to make a convincing point to the person we are engaged in conversation with. As we do this, we don't really consider how extraordinary the activity we are engaged in is. We think, but we don't really *think about thinking*. It has become automatic. Yet, this was not always the case. Early humans no doubt found cognition to be as novel and interesting as the *other* tools— 5 the tools that enhanced our physical strength—that they relied upon to increase our chances for survival in a challenging world. In other words, our early ancestors *invented* thought.

There was a symbiotic relationship between the great early technological developments of agriculture and architecture and the cognitive activity that developed, sustained and continually improved them. Our developments shaped our thinking, and our thinking shaped our developments. We see this in the laws and codes of conduct that were laid down by the leaders of the great early civilizations of Mesopotamia, Egypt and the Indus Valley. The organization and structure we had acquired through our technological lifestyle was applied to our social behavior as well. And that brings us to the great thinkers of Athens in ancient Greece.

The Greeks known as the Pre-Socratic Philosophers laid down the basic principles for logical, rational discovery and experimentation. Not as much of their writings exists as does the extensive preserved works of Plato and Aristotle. However, those more famous later philosophers built on the works of the earlier thinkers. Pre-Socratic philosophers, such as Thales and Pythagoras, were impressed by the human power to organize and construct the physical world through agriculture and architecture. They came to believe that the natural world could be understood according to its *own* organization, as if there were an "architecture" to the universe itself.

Statue of Pythagoras

This was a very different way of conceiving of nature from that of our hunter-gatherer ancestors, who didn't view nature from an observational standpoint. Hunter-gatherers didn't so much "study" nature as they simply strove to live within its confines, as all other animals did. The notion that there is nature on one hand, and a human mind that can observe it on the other, would not have arisen without our early technological developments and innovations. Tribal peoples, in other words, experienced ⁵ themselves *as* nature in such an obvious way that there was no point in moving out from there to try to understand "nature" in the abstract.

On the other hand, when people, such as those along the Nile and Indus rivers, transitioned to farming communities and 10 housed themselves within walls, a separation between man (the actor) and nature (that which is acted upon) was born. This was the *organized, structured* world that spurred the ancient Greeks (and Indians, Persians and Chinese around the same time) on to rational, logical thinking. 15

By the time we come to Aristotle, 2,500 years ago, the brain as a thinking tool was fully operational. Within his vast body of work, which spans aesthetics, astronomy and zoology, we find the first 20 known formal study of logic. Aristotle was the individual who *thought about thinking* the earliest and most rigorously. In his six texts collectively known as the *Organon*,

Statue of Aristotle

he lays out the organization and structure of logical thought sim- 25 ilarly to how an architect lays out the blueprint for a multi-storied building.

According to Aristotle, logic begins with establishing principles that can be agreed upon; for example, the sun provides heat. Rational thought proceeds from these principles by introducing 30 related propositions that can be evaluated in terms of their truth or falsehood, using the established principles as a reference point. The interplay between the established principles, the introduced propositions and the human brain's ability to challenge and either verify or refute the propositions is the "mind technology" that enables humans to continually progress.

A rather obvious way to understand the importance of this innovation is to contrast it with the way a beaver builds dams. Beavers are very accomplished builders, but a beaver dam today is no different

Beaver

from a beaver dam of five hundred thousand years ago. No principles of building are tested, and no innovations are passed on to beaver offspring. Even with human hunter-gatherer societies, we see only relatively minor modifications in tool-making, hunting activity and shelter-building over hundreds of generations.

Logic, as we have seen, gradually emerged in the centuries leading up to Aristotle, through the Pre-Socratic thinkers, to Socrates, to Plato. It culminated in Aristotle's *Organon*, which codified the rules of logic. Once it was firmly established, logical thinking enabled the human species to achieve rapid progress and expand into new fields of exploration, such as physics, medicine, finance and computing.

Mankind has used logic to achieve every great invention, development and innovation from Aristotle's time onward, culminating in the 20th century with our "thinking machines" (our calculators, our word processors, our computers, our "smart" devices) and in the 21st with the arrival of AI. And logic, let's recall, was an *invention*; a very important one along our Road to AI.

# Exercises

**A** Choose the definition of the words as they are used in the essay.

1. muse
2. symbiotic
3. extensive
4. zoology
5. culminate

a. develop to the highest level
b. the study of animals
c. think deeply
d. benefitting both sides
e. covering a large area

**B** Choose the correct answer to complete each sentence.

1. The author feels that the laws and codes of ancient civilizations
   a. made it possible for early human technology to develop rapidly.
   b. are an early indication of how technology shaped human thought.
   c. laid down the basic principles of logic and experimentation.

2. According to the author, structure and organization
   a. developed independently from agriculture and architecture.
   b. do not exist in the natural world.
   c. are elements of both technological and social developments.

3. (Choose the INCORRECT answer.) Compared to Pre-Socratic philosophers, Aristotle's works

   a. made a clearer distinction between man and nature.

   b. are better preserved.

   c. covered a greater range of topics.

C Discuss the topics.

1. The author compares human engineering to beaver dam building. Most people think that beavers build their dams according to "instinct." To what degree do you think that animals are capable of thinking, rather than just following instinct? Give reasons for your opinion.

2. The Apollo manned mission to the moon and the International Space Station are two of mankind's greatest technological achievements. What do you think were some of the basic "principles" (of Aristotelian logic) that were established in order to accomplish these achievements?

3. Aristotle lived in a time when scientific fields were so new that he was able to make progress in a wide variety of fields. Today, scientific research is highly specialized and most working scientists focus on narrow areas of study. Do you think it is possible for a "21st century Aristotle" to appear, capable of achieving breakthroughs in multiple areas of science?

# Part 2

## The Age of Inventions
### —Moving Civilization
### Forward

# Unit **6**

## A Time of Technological "Miracles" and Geniuses

 DL 058 ~ 065  CD1-58 ~  CD1-65

It's a little embarrassing to admit, but we live in an age where we know virtually nothing about the things that we use and depend on each and every day of our lives, beyond how to use them. Look around yourself, in your home and classrooms, the
5 stores where you buy things, etc. Everyone in today's world is surrounded by things we know how to use, but *not* how they work! The inner machinery of everyday items is utterly mysterious to the vast majority of people living today, especially for those of us without any type of engineering or programming training.

We can use a remote control to change the channel on our television, but we know next to nothing about, for example, how power is stored in the battery inside it (all we know is that we need to change it periodically). Nor do we know how electromagnetic signals are sent from the controller to the television, or anything at 5 all about the complex web of circuits and wires working away *behind* the screen in front of us that instantly replaces one image with another with a press of our thumb. If we were to visit a manufacturing plant and be shown a typical machine used to produce a TV, we would be even more lost! 10

Contrast this situation with a student in ancient Athens, walking down its wide streets on an early morning in 2500 BC to pick up a loaf of bread. He or she would 15 have been treated to an impressive array of sights, walking past

The Acropolis

fountains adorned with lifelike statues of Olympian gods and goddesses, and looking upward to the great architectural feats of the Acropolis, visible from all quarters of the city. Impressive 20 as all these sights were, to this ordinary citizen of Athens the statues, the buildings and the fountains were, at the same time, familiar. There was nothing very mysterious or inscrutable about them. The student recognized them all as having been created by *tools*, mostly hand-held tools. 25

Though the objects themselves were highly detailed and finely crafted, the tools used to create them were relatively crude. This was true about every tool being employed in the Athenian's world. One could recognize the purpose each one served just by looking at it, whether it was sawing, hammering, plowing, pound- 30

ing grain, etc. The skill and craftsmanship of the city's artisans were certainly admired. Nevertheless, an average citizen was aware that with the proper training, he or she would have been able to work in the same way as the masters did. It was all a
5  matter of tools and training.

Today, as was pointed out, we are surrounded by technological mysteries in a way the ancient Athenians were not. What happened?

During the European Renais-
10 sance, a profound societal transition began—from The Age of Tools (which could easily be identified and understood, and were mostly hand-held) to The Age of Inventions (which con-
15 tained hidden and often minute in-

Clavichord

ner machinery). Little by little, beginning in the homes and classrooms of the noble classes, a series of mysterious and "miraculous" inventions began to appear, one after the other. These ranged from musical instruments such as the clavichord, to useful home
20 items such as clocks, to scientific inventions like the microscope and telescope. With these inventions, one could no longer convince oneself—as our ancient Athenian student could—that with the proper tool training, one could easily create similar things. These inventions all contained mysterious inner workings of a
25 highly specialized nature.

The people who invented these mysterious machines were rare and special individuals. They were, clearly, *geniuses*. And as the world increasingly began to be shaped by geniuses and their ingenious inventions, a dramatic power shift occurred. For
30 many thousands of years, the power in society was held by the

landowners/rulers, and the priest class. The priests of past societies, whether Christian, Muslim or Buddhist, laid claim to the mysterious aspects of society. The physical, everyday world was knowable to all, but priests claimed to hold special, exclusive knowledge about the spiritual world. This gave them great power because, in all ancient societies, staying on God's good side could be the difference between a life of fortune and a life of misery (as well as an afterlife of bliss or eternal suffering!). People relied upon the priests, with their special powers and access, to tell them how to behave in order not to displease the deities they worshipped. The landowners/rulers aligned themselves with the power of the priests, so that pharaohs, kings, tsars, and emperors could claim a divine mandate to rule and enslave others.

However, as the physical world *itself* became more mysterious through an ever-growing parade of miraculous inventions, society's "geniuses"—its scientists and inventors—rapidly separated themselves from the common people by the power of their own minds. As a result, society gradually began to shift its attention away from its priests and toward its geniuses. People became fascinated by inventions like the microscope and telescope, and less interested in the mysteries beyond the physical universe that priests spoke of.

Standing above all these transformative inventions, there is one (as we will see in the next unit) that played a monumental role in bringing the priest class and landowners/rulers to their knees.

# Exercises

**A** Choose the definition of the words as they are used in the essay.

1. array                    a. large group
2. adorned                  b. decorated
3. inscrutable              c. difficult to understand
4. crude                    d. join in agreement
5. align                    e. simple and basic


**B** Choose the correct answer to complete each sentence.

1. The author uses the example of the Athenian student
   a. to show that human technology is more impressive today.
   b. to demonstrate how human intelligence has declined since ancient Greece.
   c. to depict a time when technology was familiar to the common people.

2. The Early Renaissance began an era
   a. when technology became more widely available to the common people.
   b. when inventors began to acquire power through their skill and knowledge.
   c. when landowners increased their power by aligning with priests.

3. Over time, the role of priests in society

   **a**. diminished because the priests were uninterested in technology.

   **b**. switched from focus on the spiritual world to the natural world.

   **c**. was challenged by the public's growing interest in scientific and technological developments.

## C Discuss the topics.

1. The author says it is "embarrassing" how unfamiliar we are with the mechanisms inside the devices we rely on. Do you agree? How familiar do you feel with the technology you use on a daily basis? Do you wish you understood it better? Why or why not?

2. Imagine yourself as the Athenian student in the passage. In what ways do you think his or her life would be most similar to your life as a student today? In what ways would it be most different?

3. Our modern world, where we are surrounded by amazing technology, is a result of the discoveries of many scientific geniuses throughout history. Who do you think of when you hear the word "genius"? What do you feel makes such individuals special?

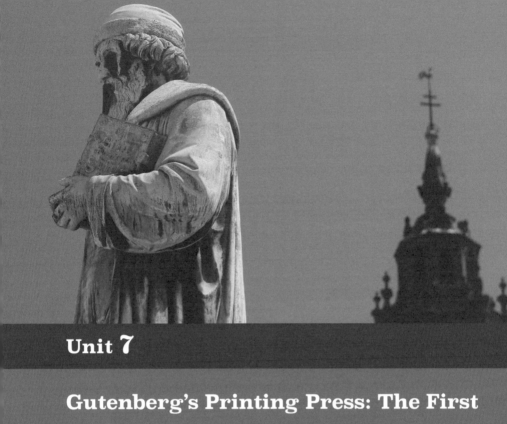

# Unit 7

# Gutenberg's Printing Press: The First Information Age

DL 066 ~ 076  CD1-66 ~ CD1-76

In mankind's ongoing relationship with technology, there are a mere handful of inventions which have been as influential as Johannes Gutenberg's printing press. Let's examine that claim.

5        Before Gutenberg, there simply weren't very many books in the world because the process of making them was exceedingly slow and painstaking. Bookmaking before Gutenberg was the job of "scribes" (which literally means people who write things by hand). The majority of these scribes were monks living in Euro-

pean monasteries. Slowly, slowly, they reproduced page after page of ancient literature, most commonly the Bible and other Christian texts (but also some of the writings of ancient Greek and Roman authors such as Plato and Herodotus). Whereas scribes almost exclusively reproduced existing works, the arrival of the 5 printing press began an explosion of new and original works, including the history-making writings of Martin Luther and Thomas Paine.

Sixty years after Gutenberg produced the world's first printed book (the *Gutenberg Bible*) in 1455, fellow German Martin Luther used the press to publish his *95 Theses* and launch the Protestant Reformation, radically trans-

The Gutenberg Bible 15

forming the world's most powerful religion. Three centuries after its invention, Thomas Paine used the press to publish *Common Sense*. This document galvanized sentiment for independence for England's North American colonies. It spearheaded the American Revolutionary War, resulting in the world's first modern democ- 20 racy. A few decades later, revolutionaries in France relied heavily on the press to spread their message of defiance against French royalty. The result was the first public uprising to bring down a monarchy, dramatically altering European, and world, history. Gutenberg and his ingenious invention changed the world. 25

Gutenberg himself had no such grand vision of transforming society. He was, simply, an inventor who had experienced both success and failure in his career until striking it rich with his printing press. He was not out to challenge the power of the priest class or the landowners/rulers. Yet, such was the power of 30 the printed word that his invention was instrumental in striking decisive blows against both the Catholic Church and the European monarchy.

The Gutenberg printing press launched the first "Information Age," making it possible for philosophical ideas about society, as well as scientific theories, to spread rapidly across Europe and North America. By enabling information to be shared and studied as never before, Gutenberg's invention made other groundbreaking inventions possible. Scholars, sci-

Statue of Charles Darwin

entists and inventors could compare notes with their contemporaries around the globe through the spread of information. This led to such breakthroughs as the European Enlightenment and Darwin's theory of evolution, as well as to new inventions such as steam locomotives and fuel-powered automobiles.

Just as the earliest technologies of Agriculture and Architecture introduced Organization and Structure into mankind's intellectual toolbox, the exchange of ideas leading to new discoveries and applications made possible by the printing press can be encapsulated in a single word: Synthesis. Synthesizing ideas and approaches, and coming up with new and innovative ways to combine different technologies has been a hallmark of the technological process ever since.

Take, for example, one of today's most ubiquitous items, the smartphone. It is an all-in-one device that combines numerous technologies that preceded it, such as telephones, video, the Internet, GPS, etc. Another example is AI, which synthesizes computing technology with neuroscience and linguistics, among other fields.

Back to Gutenberg. It is interesting to note that the printing press was, itself, a synthesis of already existing technologies. In designing his press, Gutenberg combined technologies that were already in use, some of them having been created for very different purposes than the ones he gave them. The pressing mechanism used to affix letters to paper was already being used in Europe for winemaking (where it was used to press grapes) and in the production of olive oil (where it was used to press the oil out of the fruit).

Gutenberg's Printing Press

Movable type blocks, an essential feature of the press, had been developed in China, but were in fact rarely used for lengthy texts (think of them as the *hanko* that are still commonly used in Japan today). Gutenberg soon realized that wooden or ivory blocks, which the Chinese used, easily broke under the extreme pressure the press applied. He came up with a solution. He utilized the technology of metal smelting, already a commonplace process, to produce much sturdier blocks that could be used thousands of times.

Even the ink his press used was a synthesis. Gutenberg combined ink used by scribes with tar that shipbuilders used for waterproofing to create a more permanent and durable ink, better suited to the mass production of documents.

We can think of Gutenberg's printing press as a "medieval smartphone." It was a revolutionary invention that brilliantly combined already existing technologies in a new, innovative way.

Gutenberg's press was so ingenious, and of such great benefit to mankind, that it remained the standard model for publishing books and pamphlets for nearly four centuries. It was finally replaced by William Koenig's steam powered press in the early 1800s, at which point the amount of printed material grew exponentially and daily newspapers reached millions of readers, bringing the Information Age to every corner of the earth. But it all started with Gutenberg and his invention that played such a vital role in shaping our modern world.

# Exercises

**A** Choose the definition of the words as they are used in the essay.

1. painstaking
2. groundbreaking
3. ubiquitous
4. medieval
5. exponentially

a. increasing at an accelerating speed
b. done with great care and thoroughness
c. so common as to be found everywhere
d. innovative and pioneering
e. relating to the time in Europe before the Renaissance

**B** Choose the correct answer to complete each sentence.

1. According to the author, before the printing press few original works were published because
   a. scribes were forbidden by the church to produce anything other than Bibles.
   b. the work of producing writings page by page required so much time and labor.
   c. before the printing press, it was rare for individuals to have visions of transforming society.

2. The author suggests that one of the most significant impacts of the printing press was that it
   a. was the first invention to synthesize already existing technologies.
   b. was instrumental in spreading the messages of the Protestant, American and French revolutions.
   c. made it possible for the Bible to be reproduced.

3. In the passage, the author likens the printing press to the smartphone in that
   a. both inventions combine already existing technologies.
   b. both are used to spread information widely.
   c. the smartphone has the same potential as the printing press to remain a standard model for many years.

## C Discuss the topics.

1. Besides the Protestant Reformation, the American Revolution and the French Revolution, what are some other important world events that came about partly through the spread of the printed word?

2. There is a saying, "the pen is mightier than the sword," which means that words have greater power than military might to transform society. Do you agree? What arguments could you make in support of the saying? What arguments could you make against it?

3. For hundreds of years since the printing press, books have had a special place in society and have been loved by both scholars and the common people. However, the publishing industry is now in decline due to so much information being available and free on the Internet. Do you feel that a time will come when books are no longer necessary? If so, do you think that will be a loss to civilization in some way? Why or why not?

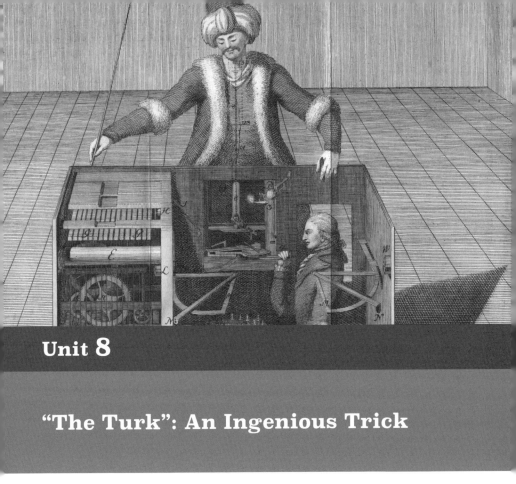

# Unit 8

## "The Turk": An Ingenious Trick

DL 077 ~ 086   CD1-77 ~ CD1-86

The Age of Inventions was an exciting time to live in. Scientists and inventors made new discoveries one after another. There seemed to be nothing the geniuses of this era weren't capable of, perhaps even unlocking the "mystery of life" itself. In this epoch, when anything seemed possible, an "invention" appeared 5 that persuaded many people that machines could be built that could think like—and even outthink—humans!

That invention, known as "The Turk," made its debut in Vienna in 1770 and rapidly captured the imagination of people throughout Europe. Common people, dignitaries, and even Napoleon himself, were fascinated. "The Turk" was an "automaton," a type of mechanical doll popular at the time that had moveable limbs, eyelids, etc. Unlike marionettes, which are manually manipulated by strings controlled by a puppeteer, automatons move mechanically. They can be made to appear to dance, draw cards from a deck, play a musical instrument, etc.

Even among such mechanical wonders, "The Turk" was special. Whereas other automatons, though they appeared lifelike, only performed automatic, mechanical tasks, "The Turk" was able to—or at least seemed to be able to—make actual decisions. To the astonishment and delight of the crowds who came to see it in theaters across the continent, it played (and usually won) games of chess!

Had mankind arrived at "artificial intelligence" 250 years ago? Of course we know the answer is no. We had centuries to go before even inventing computers, much less teaching them to make decisions on their own. Most of the people of the time, upon consideration, did not believe that "The Turk" was an actual thinking machine. There had to be (and, in fact, there was) a human being choosing the chess moves the automaton appeared to be making on its own. Yet, so ingenious and deceptive was the illusion that many who saw it in action were convinced that "The Turk" won—or at least played well—on its own.

Adopting the perspective of that earlier era, rather than our own, it shouldn't be so surprising that some people were fooled. Its inventor, Hungarian Wolfgang von Kempelen, equipped his device with an array of gears, cogs and wires that ap-

Wolfgang von Kempelen

peared quite recognizable to educated members of society at the time. They were used to seeing such mechanisms in numerous other inventions. They generally didn't know how these churning parts worked, but they knew that they *did* work, and that was enough to give "The Turk" the appearance of authenticity. 5

Moreover, to audience members moving about the machine and peering inside, there didn't seem to be any space inside for a human being to direct the movements of the mechanical chess player. It looked like a completely mechanical device.

At exhibitions, von Kempelen wound the machine up to set 10 it in motion. Gears began to whirr, and the dummy appeared to come to life. It picked up chess pieces, and carefully selected where on the board to place them. Audiences were amazed!

All that machinery, all those cogs and gears, were actually just for show, however. Indeed, there was a well-hidden human 15 inside, and it was through his chess playing skill, not the dummy's, that moves were selected. He controlled the dummy's arms and fingers via a series of levers to make it play the move he had decided upon.

Recall that this was The Age of Inventions; a time when 20 geniuses were wowing the populace with their extraordinary abilities, gradually eroding the faith that people had in the priest class, and taking on a stature somewhere between ordinary people and deities. These geniuses seemed superhuman. Thus, it was not too much of a stretch to imagine that, if they could invent ma- 25 chines that could weave clothing and play music and print books and tell time, it was within their power to invent something that could master a complicated game like chess. Mightn't the geniuses of the era have been able to "solve" the problem of thinking as they had solved so many other challenges? 30

Approximately fifty years after "The Turk's" debut, in 1818, British author Mary Shelley published her novel *Frankenstein*. This is considered the first work

5　of science fiction, and also the first known fictional portrayal of "artificial intelligence." The novel's protagonist, Victor Frankenstein, was a typical genius of the age. He invented a machine capable of

10　restoring life to inanimate human body parts, giving birth to an independently thinking monster. The story shocked readers at the time, not only for its violence but also for how frighteningly it portrayed

15　technology. *Frankenstein* and "The Turk" show that as far back as two centuries ago people had become so impressed and awed by mankind's technological prowess that they could already envision human

20　creations that could match us in thinking, and even challenge us for supremacy.

FRANKENSTEIN;

or,

THE MODERN PROMETHEUS.

IN THREE VOLUMES.

Did I request thee, Maker, from my clay
To mould me man? Did I solicit thee
From darkness to promote me?—
PARADISE LOST.

VOL. I.

London:
PRINTED FOR
LACKINGTON, HUGHES, HARDING, MAVOR, & JONES,
FINSBURY SQUARE.

1818.

Title Page of First Edition of Frankenstein, Volume I

Mary Shelley

These were only the early days of the Industrial Revolution, and mankind was already well on the Road to AI.

# Exercises

**A** Choose the definition of the words as they are used in the essay.

1. epoch                      **a**. period of time
2. dignitary                  **b**. great surprise
3. astonishment               **c**. main character
4. deceptive                  **d**. misleading
5. protagonist                **e**. important person

**B** Choose the correct answer to complete each sentence.

1. According to the author, most people of "The Turk's" era
   **a**. were quite willing to believe that inventors could create an actual thinking machine.
   **b**. did not believe "The Turk" actually made decisions, but were curious and fascinated by how convincing the illusion was.
   **c**. didn't see "The Turk" as significantly different from other "automatons" popular at the time.

2. From the passage, Wolfgang von Kempelen appears to have been
   **a**. an entertainer similar to modern day magicians.
   **b**. a fraud who tricked people in order to take their money.
   **c**. a genius inventor who challenged the power of the priest class.

3. "The Turk" and *Frankenstein* are similar in that
   **a**. both are early examples of technology being portrayed as

harmful.

**b**. both exposed inventors as having very little control over their inventions.

**c**. both reflect society's belief at the time that technology was nearing the ability to produce thinking machines.

## C Discuss the topics.

1. "The Turk" was not an actual machine capable of playing chess, but we now have computer programs which are capable of beating the most skilled chess players. What do you imagine as other ways that computers will surpass human skill levels? For example, composing music or creating artwork?

2. Mary Shelley's *Frankenstein* is seen by many as a warning about the dangers of technology. We now live in a world that has seen nuclear weapons that can destroy whole cities and great environmental damage caused by technology and industry. Do you wish that humanity had taken a more cautious approach to applying technology?

3. It is easy to look backwards and tell ourselves that we, personally, would not have been fooled by "The Turk" (and in fact, the majority of people were not). But of course we don't really know. What personality traits do you possess that would have made you skeptical about "The Turk" had you been alive at the time? What personality traits might have made you susceptible to being fooled?

# Unit 9

# The "Luddites": What Were They Fighting Against?

🎧 DL 087 ~ 097 ⊙ CD1-87 ~ ⊙ CD1-97

If you read a lot about technology, you will inevitably come across the term "Luddite." You will typically see it being used as a negative, derisive term. You will likely wonder, "what *is* a Luddite?" (and want to know how to avoid being one, since nobody in tech seems to like them). In modern usage, "Luddite" refers to a person who resists and feels threatened by technology, particularly in the way it seems to be completely taking over our lives. The term Luddite suggests people who are behind the times, and unwilling to catch up. Not to mention fighting a lost cause, as all  5 the complaining in the world has very little chance of stopping, or even slowing down, the march of technology on our Road to AI.

Where does the term itself come from? Unsurprisingly, it comes from the same era as "The Turk" and Mary Shelley's
5    *Frankenstein*. In other words, it comes from a time when people were growing increasingly awed by the power of technology while many were growing uncomfortable with just how powerful it was becoming.

The Luddites were a radical group of
10   workers in England who rebelled against the encroachment of machinery in the workplace. They saw these new industrial machines as a threat to their livelihoods and to traditional craftsmanship. They
15   took their name from Ned Ludd, a (proba-bly mythical) weaver, and heroic symbol of their movement.

The Leader of the Luddites

In 1779, in a fit of rage, Ludd broke two weaving machines in the apparel factory where he worked.
20   Although, according to the story, Ned Ludd's violent act resulted from a personal dispute with his bosses at the factory and was not intended to be an act of rebellion against industrialization, it nevertheless had the effect of inspiring the Luddites to follow his lead, and destroy machines and vandalize factories that were
25   threatening their way of life.

The Luddite Rebellion began in March 1811 in and around Nottingham, a textile manufacturing center in the English Mid-lands. When a group of laborers demonstrated for better wages, the British army was called in to break up their protest. Out-
30   raged that the government reacted to what they considered rea-

sonable demands in such a stern way, many workers took up the cause of the protestors, and the Luddite Rebellion was born.

Angry workers formed mobs that stormed factories at night, and broke the machinery inside. A common target of their ire was a machine called a stocking frame—a device they perceived as a ⁵ particularly monstrous job-stealer in that it could be operated by relatively low-skilled workers but easily outproduce skilled craftsmen.

The Luddite Rebellion last-ed for about five years, and be-came quite violent. It was said that more British soldiers were sent to crush the rebellion than were fighting Napoleon's armies overseas at the same time. Some of the leaders of the movement were hanged, and many others were killed in clashes with the military.

Statue of Napoleon

10

15

The aggressive response of the government, though horrific, was effective. Despite fears that the rebellion against modern fac-tories and new types of machinery would spread across Europe, ²⁰ it was largely contained within the region where it began, near Nottingham.

The Luddite Rebellion illustrates a fundamental difference between The Age of Tools and The Age of Inventions. When work-ing with hand-held tools, such as hammers, chisels, tongs, saws, ²⁵ etc., the difference between substandard results and masterful ones comes down to craftsmanship. Throughout the first ten thousand years of agrarian society, artisans of various fields such as farming, building and weapon-making apprenticed with mas-ter workers (the work was typically passed from father to son) for ³⁰ long periods of time, slowly developing the necessary skills to use their tools effectively. The tools themselves were simple, but the things they produced—in the hands of master craftsmen—were often stunning. As we noted earlier, such architectural marvels as the Great Pyramid at Giza, the Parthenon of Athens, and the Pantheon in Rome were built with hand-held tools manipulated by skilled artisans.

During The Age of Inventions (lasting from the Renaissance through the first stage of the Industrial Revolution), machines began to appear with mysterious hidden workings that, in many cases, were able to do things that humans, no matter how skilled, could not. The Luddites began a revolution not against technology itself, but against the technology of The Age of Inventions, which threatened to replace human labor and leave people without their livelihoods.

We see a similar discussion happening today with concerns that AI will ultimately end up eliminating human labor. As with our earlier consideration of whether agriculture was ultimately a "mistake" (Unit 3), with the Luddite Rebellion, we again see mankind questioning its relationship with technology, and weighing its costs versus its benefits. History, as the saying goes, has a way of repeating itself.

# Exercises

**A** Choose the definition of the words as they are used in the essay.

1. radical                    a. advocating dramatic change

2. rage                       b. extreme anger

3. rebellion                  c. a challenge to an organization

4. apprentice                 d. very impressive

5. stunning                   e. train under a master


**B** Choose the correct answer to complete each sentence.

1. Unlike how the term is used today, the original Luddites
   a. were violent because their hatred of technology was much stronger.
   b. achieved a great deal of success and political power.
   c. were not opposed to technology in a general sense.


2. According to the passage, Ned Ludd was
   a. a skilled craftsmen who wanted to inspire a political movement.
   b. possibly an imaginary character who was not directly involved with the Luddite movement.
   c. perhaps the first person in history to challenge the growing power of technology.


3. We can guess, based on the passage, that the Luddite Rebellion did not spread beyond the borders of England because
   a. neighboring countries were not as advanced technologically as England.

**b.** the British army acted so swiftly and violently against it.

**c.** craftsmen outside England were more receptive to working with newer machinery.

## C Discuss the topics.

1. The opposite of a "Luddite" is sometimes referred to as a "geek," meaning someone who loves technology and always wants to own the latest devices. To what degree are you a "geek" or a "Luddite" or something in between?

2. It is said that "violence is never a solution." But do you feel that the Luddites had rights that were being taken away from them by the new machines? Can you think of ways that their rebellion might have been less violent and more successful?

3. Our current era is most similar to the time of the Luddite Rebellion in the area of employment. Automation, and now AI, are gradually shrinking the types of factory jobs that employ millions of workers around the globe. What do you see as the future of labor? Do you expect factory jobs to completely disappear in your lifetime? What jobs do you imagine will replace them?

# Part 3

## The Age of Products
### —Our Manufactured World

# Unit 10

# Energy: Why the 20th Century Stands Out

DL 098 ~ 108    CD2-02 ~ CD2-12

As we journey forward on our Road to AI, let's consider the importance of energy. In Mary Shelley's novel, Frankenstein's monster was brought to life by a lightning bolt. Two hundred years ago, people recognized the potential of electricity. By the
5 middle of the 19th century, energy had begun to lay the groundwork for The Age of Products and our modern world.

Most people think of energy as coming from electricity, oil, steam, gas, coal, and more recently, nuclear energy (plus the renewable energies of solar and wind power). However, another nearly forgotten energy source—for a brief time—played a huge role in the Industrial Revolution. Nothing in the long history of human exploitation of animals quite compares to the whaling industry of the mid 18th to late 19th centuries, when

New Bedford Harbor

5

the blubber from whales was used to light city streets and homes. By the 1850s, commercial whaling had become the fifth largest industry in the United States. Its commercial center, the town of 10 New Bedford, Massachusetts, was christened "the city that lights the world."

Hundreds of thousands of whales were slaughtered—several species nearly to extinction—for the light and warmth their body fat could be converted into. In fact, whale populations shrank to 15 such dangerously low levels due to hunting that if an alternative fuel had not come about, the world would likely have experienced its first "Oil Shock" (caused by not having enough whales left to provide fat for industry) a century earlier! However, by the first decade of the 20th century, commercial whaling was all but 20 finished. With the discovery of oil in Texas in 1901, the whaling industry was eclipsed, and the most dramatic economic and technological growth the world has ever experienced began. Welcome to the 20th Century, when Oil was King!

Oil is a "fossil fuel." The history of using fossil fuels began 25 long before the 20th century. Hundreds of years ago, in the Middle Ages, people in Europe turned to coal as a heating source when timber became scarce. The people of Europe had steadily cut down the continent's forests for firewood to burn fires in their hearths for cooking, and to heat their homes. They began to mine 30 the ground for coal when the available coal on the surface became scarce, just as timber had.

The excavated mines had a problem, however. They tended to flood with rainwater, preventing workers from getting to the coal. In 1712, Englishman Thomas Newcomen came up with a solution. He invented a steam-powered pump to extract water from the mines. With his invention, two important features of the Industrial Revolution were set in place: 1) nearly unlimited access to an important *energy source* (underground coal), by means of 2) an *engine* (powered by steam).

The steam engine's design was improved about fifty years later by Scottish inventor James Watt so that it could be employed for other uses (including the steam-powered weaving machines the Luddites rebelled against half a century later). By the beginning of the 19th century, the rapidly industrializing world had coal-burning/steam-powered railway trains, ships (including the ones used for

Statue of James Watt

whale hunting), factories, etc. Gutenberg's printing press, which had been so revolutionary and important three centuries earlier, was replaced by steam-powered presses in 1814. These industrial presses much more rapidly churned out books, newspapers and magazines, giving birth to the modern publishing industry.

Let's stop to notice the progression taking place. As we have seen, for most of human history our greatest technological achievements were accomplished by manual labor. Even such engineering wonders as the Roman aqueducts and The Great Wall of China were constructed manually by tens of thousands of laborers. During most of The Age of Inventions, this remained the case. As ingenious as the new inventions were, they continued to depend on manual labor, either the pulling of the press lever in Gutenberg's printer, or the wind-

Roman Aqueducts

5

ing of clocks and automatons to set their gears in motion.

With the arrival of Watt's steam engine, inventions were supercharged. They had the power to work harder and faster, and produce on a scale never before seen. Through *energy* (coal, whale blubber, steam, and petroleum), The Age of Inventions evolved into The Age of Products (our current era).

10

Let's return to that Texas oil field. By the 1850s, petroleum's efficiency as a fuel had already made it a highly prized commodity. The steam powered engines that were being used to dig coal mines were modified into oil drilling machines, and the global search for productive oil fields was on.

15

The consolidation of the oil industry into the largest industry the world has ever known was largely achieved by one man, American John D. Rockefeller, who, unsurprisingly, became the world's first billionaire. He began his career as a refiner of "crude oil" excavated from the ground. Rockefeller and others in the early oil industry developed refining techniques that made crude oil more versatile than coal. It

20

25

John D. Rockefeller

also burned cleaner, a huge advantage as late 19th century cities were nearly choking on the smoke which coal burning caused.

30

Rockefeller was able to build success upon success, buying up oil fields in the state of Texas, which contained the largest oil reserves in the United States. He also invested in new and important uses for oil, such as gasoline, plastics and pharmaceu-
5    ticals. In effect, Rockefeller made oil the "standard currency" of the modern world. By 1910, the world, literally, ran on oil, and continues to do so more than a century later.

## Exercises

**A** Choose the definition of the words as they are used in the essay.

1. exploitation      **a.** dig deep into the ground

2. eclipse      **b.** overtake, move ahead of

3. excavate      **c.** the use of resources

4. consolidation      **d.** usable in different situations

5. versatile      **e.** the act of combining to strengthen

**B** Choose the correct answer to complete each sentence.

1. According to the author, whale fat declined as an energy source primarily because

   **a.** people began to feel that it was wrong to take the lives of so many living creatures.

   **b.** the population of whales became nearly extinct, so there was no point in hunting them any more.

   **c.** the superiority of oil as a fuel source made whale fat obsolete.

2. The passage shows how energy transformed The Age of Inventions by

   **a.** increasing its productivity by replacing manual labor with more powerful energy.

   **b.** supplying more ingenious inventions that had superior design and engineering.

   **c.** creating a variety of new occupations that workers in previous industries preferred.

3. From the passage, the most accurate statement about John D. Rockefeller is that he
   a. used his money to create a new industry: petroleum.
   b. had the vision to recognize that oil could be refined in multiple ways to achieve multiple purposes.
   c. initially experienced success in the oil industry but achieved even greater success in unrelated industries.

## C Discuss the topics.

1. From the passage, we can see that James Watt's steam engine was one of the most influential inventions in history, just as Gutenberg's printing press was. Are there similarities in how these two inventions brought about changes to our world? What do you see as the most important difference between them?

2. Japan is one of the few countries where whale hunts are still legal. As such, Japan is often criticized for continuing a practice seen as "barbaric" by much of the world. How do you feel about whale hunting? Do you feel that countries that hunted whales for energy in the past have a right to criticize Japan?

3. The world's economy has run on oil for approximately a century. However, we know that the world's oil reserves are becoming scarce, and furthermore that burning oil to run our industries damages the environment. What do you think will happen in the next one hundred years? Do you think a new energy source that is cleaner and more reliable will be able to replace oil?

# Unit 11

# The Automobile: Bridging Two Ages

DL 109 ~ 117    CD2-13 ~ CD2-21

Wherever you are reading this right now—your room, your classroom, library, etc.—take a look around for a minute. It is very unlikely that you will be able to point out more than one or two handmade items. More likely, you will not find *any*. The clothing you are wearing, frames for your glasses, the chair you are sitting on, the desk, the computer(s), pens, erasers—and this very book you are holding—have all been mass-produced. In thousands of rooms across the world, you will find exact replicas of nearly every item that fills the room you are in. As recently as

5

120 years ago, however, that would not have been the case. Before the 20th century, the majority of the items in homes, classrooms and libraries continued to be hand-crafted, one by one, just as they had been for thousands of years.

5     There is another significant feature about all the items surrounding you. *Everything*, every single object you can point to, will have spent a portion of its existence in the bed of a truck. Actually, several trucks. From factory to warehouse, from warehouse to store, probably from the store to its present location by 10 delivery van, each item in the room you are in made its way to you by way of *the automobile*, perhaps the most impactful invention in human history.

    We no longer live in The Age of Inventions. Our current era is an Age of Products, where nearly everything is mass-produced 15 in factories. If energy (steam, coal, oil, electricity) can be thought of as the bridge between these two separate eras, it is the automobile that *crossed* that bridge and brought us to our current position on the Road to AI.

    First, some history. The au- 20 tomobile began as one of the more ingenious creations of The Age of Inventions. In 1769, French inventor Nicolas Cugnot created the

A Steam-Powered Car Owned by Cugnot

first steam-powered vehicle. Much earlier, Leonardo Da Vinci— 25 The Age of Inventions' quintessential genius—had sketched the design for a spring-powered vehicle, but never produced an actual model. Clearly, cars have a long history. But from the time of Da Vinci's sketches, through Cugnot's successful model, they remained curios, not really so different from the chess playing 30 "Turk." They were an interesting way for clever humans to test their inventiveness (a hallmark of The Age of Inventions), but not much else.

So, how did this ingenious invention go from curio to ubiquitous and essential part of modern society? Firstly, we must point to the rise of fossil fuels that not only fueled the cars themselves but also the factories that produced them. However, that is, at most, only half the story. It was the *mass production* of automobiles, on assembly lines, that created the template for our modern age, in which nearly everything is produced that way.

The name most identified with automobile mass production is Henry Ford, and rightly so. European carmakers continued to use handicraft methods to build cars one at a time in small factories even as late as 1910. Some of these cars were powered by steam,

Henry Ford

some by electricity, and others by a new invention: *gasoline*, a refined petroleum product. These were beautiful, high quality cars, and some of the names of their builders are still well known today, such as (Gottlieb) Daimler and (Karl) Benz. But Henry Ford had a different vision—not only for cars, but also for manufacturing in general—and it was his vision that triumphed. It was Henry Ford who laid the cornerstone for The Age of Products.

Ford wanted to build, in his words, "a car for the masses." He saw the potential of cars becoming the dominant transportation method worldwide, connecting cities to farms (and inventing "suburbs" in the process). He also had the visionary business sense to build cars in massive numbers, *and* pay his many workers sufficient wages so that they themselves could afford to buy his economically priced cars, securing customers for his company. Furthermore, he chose to procure many car parts from outside suppliers, boosting secondary industries such as tire-making, and glass for windows and windshields.

Ford's very complete vision of modern business was duplicated in industry after industry, from radios to washing machines to refrigerators. All those mass-produced and affordable household products resulted in millions of well paid manufacturing jobs. The centuries-old system of a few very rich landowners and an overall population with little to no savings was replaced by a strong middle class who used their paychecks to fuel an ever-growing expansion of goods and services. Not only household items, but also things like annual vacations and sending ones' children to college became commonplace among the new middle class that emerged in The Age of Products.

Yet, as we have done before on our journey, we must stop to consider the downside. The car industry has been responsible for $CO_2$ emissions that threaten to raise both global temperatures and sea levels. If Henry Ford and The Age of Products have given us a century of fantastic growth, while at the same time dooming the planet, we may wonder, as we did with agriculture (and as the Luddites did), if we took an unwise path. Whether one chooses to see cars as beneficial or harmful, there is no questioning the extent to which they have shaped the modern era.

# Exercises

## A  Choose the definition of the words as they are used in the essay.

1. replica          **a**. a copy of an item
2. curio            **b**. obtain from a supplier
3. suburb           **c**. an outer area of a city
4. procure          **d**. an unusual and fascinating object
5. doom             **e**. cause to fail

## B  Choose the correct answer to complete each sentence.

1. If you were a European carmaker in the late 1890s, you were most likely to be

   **a**. working with your engineers and designers to ensure that your products maintained a reputation for high quality.

   **b**. using your revenue to increase the wages of your workers to ensure their loyalty to your company.

   **c**. developing a reliable supply chain of auto parts to decrease your manufacturing costs.

2. (Choose the INCORRECT answer.) According to the passage, Henry Ford's success came about because

   **a**. his business vision considered not only products but also treatment of employees.

   **b**. he insisted on the highest standards of quality and refined engineering.

   **c**. he aimed his cars for the mass market rather than well off customers.

3. The Age of Products can best be defined as

   a. an era in which expensive luxury items are now readily available to the masses.

   b. an era when handmade items are no longer desirable, as mass-produced items have demonstrated their superiority in numerous ways.

   c. an era where a greatly expanded middle class owns affordable, essential mass-produced items.

## C Discuss the topics.

1. The author begins the passage by pointing out just how few of the items we use on a daily basis are handmade, and how that differs greatly from earlier eras. Do you feel that mass production has caused our culture to become impersonal and excessively standardized? Explain your answer.

2. Henry Ford had a complete vision of modern life in terms of products, business and economics. Does technological and social progress depend on the chance birth of individuals (such as Ford, Thomas Edison, etc.), or is it an inevitable process that occurs without relying on specific individuals?

3. Some people have suggested that as The Age of Products is replaced by The Age of AI, it will be possible to surround ourselves with less standardized goods. They imagine individuals working with AI to design unique, personal and highly specialized things to use and enjoy. Do you think this scenario will occur in your lifetime? If so, what kinds of things would you like to "invent" with the assistance of AI?

# Unit 12

# How Mass Media Shaped Our Ideas About AI

DL 118 ~ 128　　CD2-22 ~ CD2-32

Projections about the impact of AI on society diverge into two extremes. Some believe that it will become so powerful that it will behave like the wish-granting genie of *Aladdin*. Others, including prominent people such as (late) physicist Stephen Hawking and inventor Elon Musk, warn about a far darker future for　5 humanity, with a malevolent AI in control of the world.

If the scenarios sound like heaven and hell, that might not be a coincidence. Recall that as humanity transitioned out of The Age of Tools and into The Age of Inventions, the power of the priest class diminished. As people began to tune out the priests and turn their attention to geniuses and their inventions, they focused more on the present world and less on mythical worlds of rewards or punishments.

That doesn't mean those myths went away, however. An all-powerful being deciding our eternal fate is a compelling belief. As the inventions of scientific geniuses became ever more powerful, it started to seem like perhaps they, and not the priests, might eventually deliver a non-divine but still all-powerful being, created by humans themselves! Many believe that AI's ultimate destiny is to become just such a being.

For hints about how the transference of worship from mythological deities to human technology may have come about, let's now consider electronically transmitted *mass media*: radio, television, film, recording, the Internet, etc.—a prominent feature of The Age of Products (and thus an inescapable feature of our everyday lives).

First, recall that, with Mary Shelley's *Frankenstein*, the idea of a technological monster turning against its creator was born. In 1818, when the novel was published, technological progress was proceeding so rapidly that it brewed disquiet among people of the time. This disquiet was expressed in *Frankenstein* in the form of a nightmarish monster. Fifty years after its publication, electricity—which had provided the spark of life to the monster in *Frankenstein*—was being used to light city streets and provide power to automobiles and factories (though not, thankfully, to bring

Guglielmo Marconi

82

the dead back to life!). At the same time, brilliant inventors like Thomas Edison and Guglielmo Marconi devised ways by which electricity could be used to record and transmit sounds and images, and *mass media* was born.

Imagine what these early years of mass media were like. People were, for the first time, able to hear voices disconnected from bodies and see giant images of men and women flashing on a screen. Imagine how *otherworldly* the experience was in the beginning! Technology was making "miracles" happen.

Italian opera tenor Enrico Caruso, considered the world's greatest opera singer (possessing the "voice of an angel") was the first mass media star. In 1902, via Edison's phonograph machine, Caruso's voice entered people's homes, as if from another world. Entertainment such as this had never existed before. Society created a new class of semi-mythical beings, called "stars," suggesting they, like mythical beings, came from the sky.

Thomas Edison and His Early Phonograph

In 1905, the first movie theaters opened in the United States. Enthralled audience members seated themselves in dark, church-like chambers and saw *huge* faces on the screen, two or three meters high, with glowing, silver skin. Silent film stars, like Rudolph Valentino, Lillian Gish and Charlie Chaplin, didn't speak; they conveyed powerful emotions through their expressions. They appeared magical and otherworldly, nearly god-like. People of the early 20th century could—*electronically*—fill their homes with the "voices of angels" and visit enchanted movie pal-

5

10

15

20

25

30

aces to see silvery giants love and battle on screens. Through mass media, technology began building its own mythology to replace what had nearly disappeared with the fall of the priest class. And people devoured these new myths as if subconsciously recognizing something had been missing from their lives.

Interestingly, mass media depicted technology from very early on, shaping the public's views of it. In 1902, French director Georges Méliès created *A Trip to the Moon*, the first sci-fi film. It depicted a rocket ship and a successful moon landing.

AI has frequently been portrayed, usually as a villain, in entertainment. In 1927, Fritz Lang directed the full-length film *Metropolis*, which presented film's first image of a robot (one that looks very similar to the C-3PO character in *Star Wars*). "She" is malevolent, and leads a murderous rebellion. *Frankenstein* was made into a popular movie in 1931. Stanley Kubrick's film *2001: A Space Odyssey* (1968) features a conscious, super-intelligent computer that takes over a spaceship and murders the crew. For contrast, we have the lovable "droids" of the *Star Wars* series (which began in 1977), but we also have the malevolent AI over-lords of *The Terminator* (1984) and *The Matrix* (1999).

Our ideas of AI as all-powerful and superhuman are largely shaped by these mass media portrayals. Thus, as news stories predicting an AI "Singularity" proliferate, we must ask ourselves how much is based on actual science, and how much is based on the age-old—and recently modernized—human tendency to my-thologize.

# Exercises

**A** Choose the definition of the words as they are used in the essay.

1. diverge          **a**. gods
2. malevolent     **b**. related to cultural legends and stories
3. mythical         **c**. evil
4. deities           **d**. go in opposite directions
5. enthralled      **e**. fascinated

**B** Choose the correct answer to complete each sentence.

1. The author suggests that it "might not be a coincidence" that
   **a**. people became more interested in geniuses than priests during The Age of Inventions.
   **b**. predictions about future AI powers are similar to religious depictions of the afterlife.
   **c**. it is scientists and inventors like Stephen Hawking and Elon Musk who are most concerned about AI being used in harmful ways.

2. The "disquiet" the author refers to when discussing Mary Shelley's *Frankenstein*
   **a**. resulted from concerns that technology was growing so powerful that humans risked losing control over it.
   **b**. was created by Mary Shelley in order to frighten her readers about the power of technology.
   **c**. arose from a fear among the populace that electricity had tremendous destructive power.

**3.** The author suggests that the great devotion audiences exhibited toward mass media "stars"

    **a.** reflects an innate worshipful quality in humans that had previously been fulfilled through religious practices.

    **b.** demonstrates that audiences were more interested in the technological methods of presenting entertainment than the performances themselves.

    **c.** resulted in the huge demand for science fiction themes in popular entertainment as well as the desire to see AI portrayed in it.

## C Discuss the topics.

**1.** We take mass entertainment for granted now, having grown up with it. However, as the author points out, the earliest audiences reacted to it with the awe that comes from seeing something completely new. Can you think of any types of future entertainment (made possible by new technology) that might have the same effect on you? What is the most amazing future entertainment you can imagine?

**2.** The passage comments upon the extreme amount of devotion that many fans feel toward entertainment and its stars. In Japan, this is particularly evident in the "idol" phenomenon. Why do you think young people become so devoted to girl/boy groups and pop singers? Do you think the devotion is too extreme in some instances?

**3.** The author suggests that it is perhaps ancient human myths about heaven and hell that cause us to imagine a nearly omnipotent AI with powers to reward or punish us. Do you think predictions about the future power of AI are based more in actual science, or in human psychology (or a combination of the two)? Discuss why you think so.

# Part 4

## The Age of AI
### —Pushing the Boundaries

# Unit 13

# The Computer: Moonshots and Desktops

DL 129 ~ 140    CD2-33 ~ CD2-44

In 1819, British engineer Charles Babbage matched his chess skills against "The Turk" (Unit 8) and lost, twice. Since debuting in 1770, "The Turk" had become an international sensation, and was still going strong when Babbage measured his
5   chess prowess against it. Babbage may have lost his matches, but he "won" in another way. He came away fully convinced (as we have already confirmed) that the machine was a clever hoax. Thus, he recognized that no inventor had yet actually created a thinking machine. Rather than spend his energy trying to expose

the machine as a fraud, Babbage took inspiration from it. He asked himself, what *would* a thinking machine be like? By what mechanisms could a machine be taught to think? More than 200 years ago, the Road to Technology was already pointed toward computers. 5

Partnering with mathematician Ada Lovelace in the 1830s, Babbage set about inventing the world's first computational machine. Their concept of an "Analytical Engine" included standard components of modern computers like memory storage capacity and programmability. Lovelace's vision was even more for- 10 ward-looking than Babbage's. Foreseeing AI, she imagined the Analytical Engine being able to compose its own music!

Unable to secure fund- ing to complete their project, Babbage and Lovelace's ma- chine was left unfinished by the time of Babbage's death in 1871. But the copious notes he made for both the Analyt- ical Engine and its predeces- sor, which he called a "Difference Engine," were instrumental in launching the modern computer era. 15

Difference Engine
20

It would be more than one hundred years after Babbage began planning his computing machines that the first fully func- tioning computer, the ENIAC, began operating in the United 25 States in 1946. Coming a year after the end of WWII, comput- ers—although they would have no doubt afforded a tremendous advantage to countries that employed them—did not play a sig- nificant role in that conflict. They did, however, play a major role in the war's aftermath. 30

After successfully exploding hydrogen bombs, which were much more powerful than even the atomic bombs used at the very end of WWII, Cold War rivals the United States and the Soviet Union faced a problem. Both militaries already had a stock
5  of weapons powerful enough to destroy all life on earth. There really wasn't much tactical or psychological advantage in continuing to simply make weapons even *more* powerful.

So, they needed a new frontier upon which to battle for technological supremacy, and the "space race" was born. The two
10  superpowers set about competing at the most scientifically challenging endeavor ever attempted by mankind—the exploration of outer space—and they needed computers to help them win.

The computers both countries used to make the millions of calculations necessary to lift rockets out of the earth's atmo-
15  sphere, reach their target and return, *and* sustain the life of passengers, were enormous. They filled whole rooms and were run by dozens of engineers and technicians.

The Soviets won the first round, successfully completing
20  an orbit around Earth in their *Sputnik 1* in 1957. However, it was the United States that garnered the biggest prize by successfully sending a team of
25  astronauts to the moon, and

Apollo 11 Command Module "Columbia"

safely back, with the *Apollo 11* mission, completed in July 1969. In the process of "winning" (actually, both sides have grounds for claiming victory) the space race, American computer scientists laid the groundwork for today's Internet with the development
30  of a network computing system known as ARPANET. ARPANET

began modestly, linking research departments at a mere four U.S. universities, but by the 1980s, the "worldwide web" that grew out of it was well on its way to linking hundreds of millions of people and changing our world.

The Apollo moon mission achieved something else. It in- 5 spired a young generation of technologically savvy teenagers and pre-teens to fall in love with computers. The average age of the engineers, technicians and programmers who worked on the Apollo mission at the time of the moon landing was only 26. Many had begun working for NASA in their late teens. 10

In the late 1960s, bright American kids witnessed a group of young geniuses work together and seemingly achieve the impossible. If we can put a man on the moon, they wondered, what *else* might humans and tech-

Steve Jobs

Bill Gates

15

nology achieve together? Two of these young men's names you 20 have no doubt heard of: Steve Jobs and Bill Gates.

Let's recall that up until that time, computers were large, taking up whole rooms, mostly being used by large organizations, such as research laboratories, large companies, government offices, universities, etc. As such, throughout the 1960s, computers 25 did not fit comfortably into The Age of Products. They were not mass-produced, and were not available to households the way cars, refrigerators and televisions were.

Jobs and Gates were part of a generation that had grown up surrounded by everyday technology. As children of The Age of 30

Products who had fallen in love with computers, they were deter-
mined to make them ubiquitous, as Henry Ford had done seven
decades earlier with cars. Jobs and Gates, and the companies
they started—Apple and Microsoft—succeeded in making the
5    *personal computer* an item for the home, and eventually a car-
ry-around item. And that takes us nearly all the way along the
Road to AI. Just one more stop to go...

# Exercises

**A** Choose the definition of the words as they are used in the essay.

1. fraud       **a.** a fake that is intended to trick
2. predecessor       **b.** well informed and knowledgeable
3. frontier       **c.** something that came before
4. modestly       **d.** territory
5. savvy       **e.** unimpressively

**B** Choose the correct answer to complete each sentence.

1. Charles Babbage's encounter with "The Turk"
   **a.** impressed upon him the need to quickly create a thinking machine before potential rivals could.
   **b.** provided him with insights into the type of machinery necessary to build a thinking machine.
   **c.** challenged him to seriously consider the attributes of a true thinking machine.

2. According to the author, the "space race"
   **a.** became necessary because the United States and the Soviet Union needed to create employment opportunities for scientists and engineers who had previously worked in the military.
   **b.** had multiple markers for success, such that both superpowers felt they had legitimate claims to victory.
   **c.** was undertaken as the two superpowers recognized the need to expand their military capabilities to outer space.

**3.** Compared to cars and refrigerators, computers were a late-comer to mass production because

    **a.** computing technology came about much later.

    **b.** they began as products primarily for use by large organizations and thus demand for them was limited.

    **c.** there were no true pioneers in the computer industry before Steve Jobs and Bill Gates.

## C Discuss the topics.

**1.** Although "The Turk" did not contain an actual computer, the passage shows how it still played a role in the development of computers. Do you think that the inspiration provided by non-scientific fields such as music, art, fiction, entertainment, etc., is essential to the development of technology? Why or why not?

**2.** From the passage, we learn that computers did not play a major role in the last major global war, but they will certainly be a decisive strategic factor if "World War Three" is ever fought. What are your concerns about AI—perhaps the most powerful technology ever developed by humans—being used in wartime? Can anything be done to prevent that?

**3.** According to the passage, the "space race" began as a rivalry between two global superpowers. However, now, with projects such as the International Space Station, the emphasis is on cooperation among countries and the sharing of technology. What do you see as the ultimate potential of space development? Does it have the potential to lead to peace on Earth?

# Unit 14

# Data: Big, Bigger, Biggest

🎧 DL 141 ~ 147   🔘 CD2-45 ~ 🔘 CD2-51

    We've come a long way on our journey. Let's return briefly
to the baby on the train we met in Unit 1. Her brain's growth
requires a flow of incoming stimuli. It is constantly taking in
information about the world, storing significant portions of that
input as memory, processing it, and making connections between    5
new input and stored input. The baby then turns this input into
knowledge because the human brain is an extraordinary instrument for doing just that. We call it "learning," and it requires
both the instrument (in our case, the human brain) and the input

(the stimuli the brain receives and processes). Recently, mankind has begun teaching *its* "baby" (the computer) to learn and grow, just as our own brains do. We call this "artificial intelligence," or AI. And the input AI requires is called "data."

5     From our earliest days as an agrarian species, data has played an important role in society (although the term itself was not coined until the 1600s and not widely used until recently). Farming societies needed to calculate the crop yields of the land they farmed. They needed to keep records in order to know the
10 best time to plant to achieve the best harvest. They needed to know how many tons of seed to hold in reserve for the next season's planting, and also how many to keep in reserve should a harvest fail, in order to avoid famine.

    So, data—facts and sta-
15 tistics collected together for reference and analysis—have been a part of human society since we first began our Road to AI. However, data didn't
20 explode to a size capable of enabling AI to imitate human  thought until quite recently. Furthermore, an important reason why it did explode—and become *Big Data*—is that The Age of Products created a new and valuable role for nearly every human
25 on the planet, child to centenarian: *the consumer*.

    When society transitioned from The Age of Inventions to The Age of Products—roughly the time Ford began selling his Model T—companies began engaging in competition on a scale far beyond anything that had come before. In fact, they engaged in a
30 type of warfare similar to that engaged in by countries.

98

Whereas countries tend to go to war over resources, companies compete for you and me. We, the consumers, are the prize. One company's gain is another company's loss. To gain new customers and avoid losing old ones, companies need to thoroughly understand consumer behavior. They need to know why people choose the products they do, what satisfies them about these products, and what would make them even *more* satisfied in the future, so they will remain loyal. This is called "consumer research," and it yields an enormous amount of data.

Consumer research traces its origins to government census-taking. Particularly in the United States—because it was a country that expanded rapidly both in terms of geography and population—census-taking was a vital government activity. Census forms containing questions about households for citizens to answer were taken from home to home by census takers. Company executives quickly realized that the same methodology could be used to ask shoppers about products—ones they used, ones they rejected, or ones they would like in the future, etc.—in order to hold a strategic advantage over their competitors. Consumers, either in their homes or in stores, were asked to spend a few minutes filling out a questionnaire about their preferences, receiving a small gift in return, such as a bag of coffee or a coupon. As computers came more and more into use by large companies in the 1960s and 1970s, the information about consumer behavior was stored in their computers' *databases*. What we now refer to as Big Data began to emerge.

But that was only the beginning. Today, with the ubiquity of the smartphone, mountains of data are being generated every second by billions of people all over the world. This data doesn't just help companies sell products any longer. It is being fed into

ingenious AI systems to help
them grow "smarter" all the
time. Every time you make a
purchase online, snap a "selfie"

5   or even mention an activity
such as taking a vacation
while chatting with a friend
on your smartphone, you are helping computers get smarter.
Like a baby, they are learning about the world from all the input
10  that each of us provides them. Every year, they know us better,
and become more like us. Soon, they will drive cars more safely
and energy-efficiently than we do, and the idea of a car that can't
drive on its own will eventually seem as odd as a car without
seatbelts. These emerging intelligent systems will solve climate
15  change problems better than we do. They will predict the fluctuations of stock markets *much* better than we do. They will transition us out of The Age of Products and into The Age of AI.

# Exercises

**A** Choose the definition of the words as they are used in the essay.

1. stimuli          **a.** things that generate activity
2. famine           **b.** giving reliable support
3. loyal            **c.** changes
4. vital            **d.** a period of food scarcity
5. fluctuations     **e.** necessary

**B** Choose the correct answer to complete each sentence.

1. The passage explains that data
   **a.** took on a new role in The Age of Products.
   **b.** has always been necessary in society but wasn't recognized as being important until the 1600s.
   **c.** has exploded recently primarily because of advances in AI.

2. The United States undertook censuses
   **a.** in order to assist American companies in collecting information about potential customers.
   **b.** because its rapid growth in both population and land made it necessary to keep records.
   **c.** because the early era of computing revealed that information gained from them would become vital.

3. (Choose the best comparison) According to the passage, Big Data is to AI
   **a.** what seeds are to agriculture.
   **b.** what paintbrushes are to a painting.

**c.** what a textbook is to a student.

## C Discuss the topics.

1. It has been said that in the current era, where many applications and other services are "free," the actual product is "us." In other words, the information that we voluntarily provide to tech companies by using their technology is how they make their money. Do you feel this is true? How comfortable/uncomfortable are you about being a "product"?

2. In The Age of Products, people generally play two roles: earners (through their jobs) and consumers (through their purchases). Both roles are necessary to keep economies running. Compare the two roles in terms of their importance. Does one appear more necessary than the other to you? Explain why or why not.

3. The passage explains how, as Big Data continues to accumulate, the capabilities of AI will greatly expand. Do you think there might come a time in the future when AI "knows" us better than we know ourselves, and will be able to make better choices for us in terms of food, medicine, exercise, and even romantic relationships and marriage? Discuss how you would feel about such a scenario if it were to come about.

# Unit 15

# How Far Will AI Take Us?

DL 148 ~ 154    CD2-52 ~ CD2-58

Our Road to AI has brought us to the present moment. Now, let's look ahead to the future and try to imagine where this powerful new technology will take us. We have looked at various technological developments throughout history in order to show how AI fits along a continuum of progress as the next important breakthrough along a road that goes back far into the past. As with agriculture, the printing press and the automobile, AI's impact is certain to be huge and bring about as yet unanticipated changes to society.

Should we fall for the idea that AI will soon become conscious, and shortly thereafter make exponential leaps above human intelligence to become a god-like being that will either fulfill our ancient longing for heaven or our similarly ancient fear of hell? And do this within our lifetimes (futurist and inventor Ray Kurzweil has famously given 2045 as the year when AI surpasses human intelligence—a point he refers to as "The Singularity"— and begins creating on its own)? Probably not. As was suggested in Unit 12, such ideas are more likely science fiction rather than actual science. However, AI *is* going to change the world to a degree that only a handful of inventions and developments have done in the past. What can we expect to see on the horizon?

● New Economics

AI is already disrupting the world of work. From the time of Henry Ford's Model T, a robust middle class with well-paying jobs has fueled demand for products and services. This has resulted in global economic expansion that has lifted millions of people in both the developed and developing worlds out of poverty. Demand for the big items in The Age of Products: cars, televisions, refrigerators, computers, etc., created jobs for *people*. In The Age of AI, on the other hand, we can expect to see job shrinkage, as more and more tasks will be taken over by AI. We will probably see a Universal Basic Income (UBI) distribution system emerge as most of the work of society transfers from people to AI. UBI will enable hundreds of millions of people who no longer work to afford necessities while society adjusts to the new reality of a nearly "jobless" economy until new roles for people to fill can be created.

● Robots, LOTS of Robots

Robots will become as ubiquitous in The Age of AI as cars and trucks are in The Age of Products. Some will be designed to look and behave as close to humans as possible, and we will interact with  them in stores, hotels, hospitals, and so on. Others will look and behave like children's beloved anime and movie characters. They 10 will not only entertain, but will also be useful as educational tools and even bodyguards for children. If you are in your teens as you read this now, get ready for your grandchild (or possibly even your child) demanding such a robot, perhaps a Doraemon or an R2D2, for Christmas! 15

● Climate Change

One of the biggest challenges the world faces right now is climate change, and the most sophisticated technology mankind has ever developed is AI, so it is inevitable that the latter will 20 play an important role in mitigating the former. However, we must avoid the overly optimistic attitude that AI will do for us what we have proven unable or unwilling to do for ourselves. Climate change is *our* problem, not AI's, and it is ultimately up to us to fix what we have broken. Nevertheless, AI will be very useful 25 in terms of predicting changes in weather patterns, helping us use fuel more efficiently, deal with natural disasters and disease outbreaks more effectively, etc. We will rely on AI's superior analytical power to adjust to a more volatile natural world.

## ● "Smart" Homes/Cities

What we now call IoT (Internet of Things) will expand to the point where nearly all of our everyday sur-  roundings will be "smart" (i.e., equipped with AI and inter- acting with humans on a con-
tinual basis). "Smart" roads in cities will prevent traffic jams. Our "smart" homes will place orders for groceries and medicine which will make their way to our refrigerators and medicine cabinets with very little effort on our part (especially if 3D printers reach the capability of producing everything we need—which appears likely at some point). Much as mother's milk contains nourish- ment that helps a nursing infant resist colds, our "smart" society will be responsive to our needs at both micro and macro levels, continually calculating optimum energy usage, peak-efficiency distribution and transportation channels, water and food safety, etc.

Our descendants will live in a very different world than we do, just as we in the 21st century live in a very different world from our ancestors in pre-industrial times, and they lived in a world very different from their ancestors in pre-agricultural times. The arc of technology will continue to extend far forward into the future, in surprising and astonishing ways.

# Exercises

**A**  Choose the definition of the words as they are used in the essay.

1. continuum    **a**. lessen the impact

2. robust    **b**. involving sudden and unpredictable change

3. shrinkage    **c**. reduction

4. mitigate    **d**. progressive movement in one direction

5. volatile    **e**. strong

**B**  Choose the correct answer to complete each sentence.

1. Regarding AI, the author is

   **a**. confident that it will dramatically transform human life but skeptical that it will surpass human intelligence.

   **b**. more concerned about AI's potential to do harm than enthusiastic about its potential to do good.

   **c**. largely in agreement with Ray Kurzweil and other futurists who predict a future "Singularity" event.

2. According to the passage, one key difference between The Age of Products and The Age of AI is that

   **a**. the former has been harmful to the environment while the latter will not be.

   **b**. in the former the products we use are developed by people while in the latter most of them will be developed by AI.

   **c**. in the former, production is directly linked to employment, while in the latter this may not be the case.

3. Based on the section titled "Smart" Homes/Cities, the best definition of "smart" is
   a. able to respond to changing situations and take actions to bring about desirable results.
   b. able to take over everyday duties so that humans can focus on more interesting activities.
   c. able to convincingly mimic human thought and make decisions in the same manner as humans.

## C Discuss the topics.

1. Some people fear that AI will take most jobs away, while others say that AI will result in new types of employment opportunities, as technological innovations have traditionally done (i.e., printing press, steam engine, automobile, computers). What are your thoughts on this? What types of new jobs can you imagine?

2. If the "smart" technology of IoT combines with 3D printing in the future, it may be possible for future people to never leave their homes! Things will be ordered, paid for and "printed" all inside the home. What do you think of such a lifestyle? Does it seem "too" convenient to you? Why or why not?

3. The author suggests that AI will play a vital role in helping to address environmental issues such as climate change, deforestation and ocean acidification. These environmental concerns seem to grow more worrisome every year. Do you think AI can develop quickly enough to prevent environmental catastrophe?

# Notes

## Unit 1  Introduction: How Far Can Tech Take Us?

**page line**

10　5　**peek-a-boo**　「いないいないばあ」

11　2-　**with a straight face**　「真顔で」

　　5　**astounding**　「びっくり仰天するような」

　　8　**immortality**　「不死」

　　10　**For ~**　「～なので」

　　12　**rational**　「道理をわきまえた、まともな」

　　16　**trajectory**　「通った道筋、過程」

　　18　**breakthrough**　「大躍進」

　　19　**genome**　「ゲノム」

　　20　**crack the code**　「暗号を解読する」

　　24　**centenarian**　「100 歳以上の人」

　　29-　**An everyday item that we take for granted, such as a smartphone or a car's GPS system, would have been considered impossible a hundred years ago.**　「スマートフォンや車の GPS システムなど、我々が当たり前と考えている日常のアイテムも、100 年前だったら不可能だと考えられたことだろう」　この would は仮定法の用法。a hundred years ago の副詞句に仮定の意味が込められている。

12　6　**in a matter of days**　「およそ数日間で」

　　6-　**Along they came, one after the other, these miraculous inventions of the 20th century**　「次から次へと、これらの 20 世紀の驚くべき発明品が登場した」　Along they came は They came along の倒置されたもの。these miraculous inventions of the 20th century は、電話、車、ラジオ、冷蔵庫、テレビ、飛行機、コンピューターを表している。

　　9　**Not to mention ~**　「～は言うまでもなく」

　　10　**eradicate**　「～を撲滅する」

　　22　**surpass**　「～に勝る」

　　29　**nightmarish**　nightmare「悪夢」の形容詞形で「悪夢のような」

　　　　**enslave**　「～を奴隷にする」

13　1　**utopian**　「ユートピア的な」

　　2　**dystopian**　「反ユートピアの」

　　3　**futurist**　「人類の進歩を信じる人」

　　　　**posit**　「～を仮定する」

　　4　**"Singularity" event**　「特異点」　この具体的内容は the exact point when computers overtake humans in all forms of intelligence and then rapidly move beyond us「コンピュータがあらゆる形式の知性において人類を凌駕し、急速に我々の先に進む時点」に具体的に記されている。

8 **close in on ~** 「～に近づく、～に迫る」

12 **fact** 「事実」 実際に生じた具体的事実の場合には可算名詞となるが、fiction との対比で使われているここでの用法は不可算名詞である。

18- **retrace** 「～を再びたどる」

19- **over millennia** 「何千年にもわたって」


# Unit 2 Extending Both Muscle Power and Brainpower

**page line**

16　6　**an "Einstein"** 人名の Einstein に an がついて an Einstein となると、「アインシュタインのような人物」の意味になる。

17　4　**hominid** 「ヒト科の動物」

8　**arrowhead** 「矢じり」

17　**ran all the others** ここでは ran all the other tools と言い換えられ、「他のすべての道具を使いこなしていた」の意味。

18　**jumpstart** 「～を活性化する」

27　**giving rise to civilization** これは分詞構文で、and gave rise to civilization と書き換えられ、「文明を生み出した」の意味。

29　**Tool use enabled us to develop a skill** 直訳をすると「道具の使用は、我々がある技術を発展させることを可能にした」となるが、「道具を使うことで、我々がある技術を発展させることができた」のように訳出するとよい。

18　2　**considered the most important early technological development** consider A B で「A を B と考える」。ここでは「最も重要な初期の技術的発達と考えられる」の意味。

10　**hunter-gatherer** 「狩猟採集生活者」

11　**hoe** 「くわ」

**plow** 「すき」

16　**organized topography** ここでは「農業ができるように地形を整えた」の意味。

**furrow** 「あぜの溝」

**irrigation channel** 「用水路」

19　13　**durable** 「もちのよい、耐久性のある」 名詞形の duration は持続期間の意味で、duration of flight（航続期間）のように使う。

**why** 間投詞として「ええっと」

14　**Giza** 「ギザ」 エジプトカイロ付近のナイル川に臨む町。ピラミッドとスフィンクスで知られる。

17-　**in rapid succession** 「矢継ぎ早に」

19　**All the while** 「その間ずっと」

111

# Unit 3  Agriculture: A Mistake?

20　**depict**　「〜を描写する」

22　**recklessly**　「結果を顧みないで、無責任に」

25　**genie**　「精霊（特にランプや瓶に閉じ込められていて、呼び出した者の願い事をかなえるという精霊）」　ここではテクノロジーが精霊に例えられていて、一度その恩恵を受けたらテクノロジーがない状態には戻れないということを述べている。

# Unit 4　Architecture: Building Upward

**page line**

28　1　**tremendous**　「素晴らしい」

　　7　**Chrysler Building**　「クライスラービルディング」　ニューヨーク市マンハッタンにあるクライスラー社所有の 77 階建てのビル。

　　8　**legendary**　「有名な、伝説的な」

　　9　**skyline**　「空を背景とする輪郭」

29　2　**Empire State Building**　「エンパイアステートビルディング」　ニューヨーク市のマンハッタン区にある 102 階建てのビル。テレビ塔を含めると 443m の高さ。

　　5　**distinction**　「栄誉」

　　6　**besting**　「〜を出し抜いて、〜を負かして」　ここでは best が動詞として使われている。

　　　**Eiffel Tower**　「エッフェル塔」　パリにある鉄塔（320m）。

　　8-　**inhabitable**　「人が住める」

　10-　**diligently**　「一生懸命に、精を出して、こつこつと」

　11　**go about ~**　「〜をせっせと行う」

　18　**spire**　「尖塔」

　27　**dweller**　「住人、居住者」

30　7　**predecessor**　「先輩、先祖」

　　8　**weather-resistant**　「厳しい気候条件に耐える、耐候性の」

　11　**address**　「〜を扱う、〜を処理する」

　　　**ingenious**　「発明の才に富む」

　13　**elements**　「暴風雨」

　17　**fatality**　「（事故・戦争などによる）死、死者」

　20　**collapse**　「崩れる、崩壊する」

　23　**sturdy**　「頑強な」

　28　**footing**　「土台、基礎」

　29　**tier**　「層」

　30　**column**　「柱、円柱」

　　　**vault**　「アーチ形天井」

　30-　**suspension pylon**　「橋などを吊り下げておくための鉄塔」

31　1-　**improvise**　「即興で作る」

# Unit 5 Building Better Brains: Technology and Thinking

page line

| | 18 | **operational** 「稼働している」 |
|---|---|---|
| | 18- | **vast body of work** 「莫大な量の全著作」 |
| | 19 | **span** 「(活動・領域などが)〈～の範囲〉に及ぶ」 |
| | | **aesthetics** 「美学」 |
| | 20 | **astronomy** 「天文学」 |
| | 23 | **rigorously** 「厳密に」 |
| | 24 | ***Organon*** 「オルガノン」 アリストテレスの論理学的著作の総題。 |
| | 25 | **lay out ~** 「～を述べる、～を提示する」 |
| | 26 | **blueprint** 「(詳細な) 計画、青写真、設計図」 |
| 38 | 1 | **proposition** 「命題」 |
| | | **evaluate** 「～を評価する」 |
| | 2 | **reference point** 「評価 (判断) 基準」 |
| | 3 | **interplay** 「相互作用」 |
| | 5 | **verify** 「～が正しいことを確かめる」 |
| | | **refute** 「～の誤りを証明する、～を論駁する」 |
| | 15 | **offspring** 「子孫」 |
| | 19- | **Socrates** 「ソクラテス (470?–399 BC)」 古代アテネの哲学者。 |
| | 21 | **codify** 「～を成文化する」 |
| | 26 | **onward** 「先へ、進んで」 |

# Unit 6 A Time of Technological "Miracles" and Ge-niuses

**page line**

| | 42 | 1 | **embarrassing** 「恥ずかしい、ばつの悪い」 |
|---|---|---|---|
| | | 7 | **machinery** 「(機械の) 可動部分」 |
| | 43 | 2 | **know next to nothing** 「ほとんど知らない」 |
| | | 4 | **periodically** 「定期的に」 |
| | | | **electromagnetic** 「電磁気の」 |
| | | 6 | **circuit** 「(電気の) 回路」 |
| | | | **wire** 「電線」 |
| | | | **work away** 「せっせと働き続ける」 |
| | | 15- | **He or she would have been treated to an impressive array of sights** 「学生は印象的なずらりと並んだ名所でもてなされたことであろう」 |
| | | 18 | **lifelike** 「生きているような、真に迫った」 |
| | | | **Olympian** 「オリンポス (Olympus) の」 |
| | | 19 | **feat** 「手柄、偉業」 |
| | | 20 | **Acropolis** 「(アテネの) アクロポリス」 パルテノン神殿の所在地。 |
| | | | **quarter** 「(都市の) 地域」 |
| | | 20- | **Impressive as all these sights were** 「これらすべての名所は深い感銘を与えるものであったが」 |

# Unit 7　Gutenberg's Printing Press: The First Information Age

|  | sentiment 「気運」 |
|---|---|
| 19 | spearhead 「〜の先頭に立つ」 |
| 20 | Revolutionary War 「革命戦争」 1775–83 年の独立戦争。 |
| 22 | defiance 「反抗の態度」 |
| 23 | uprising 「反乱、暴動」 |
| 24 | monarchy 「君主制、君主政治」 |
| 26 | grand vision 「壮大な展望」 |
| 28 | strike it rich 「思わぬ大成功を収める」 |

50 1 instrumental 「助けになって」

2 decisive 「決定的な、決め手となる」

14- contemporary 「同時代の人」

16 breakthrough 「大きな進歩、貴重な新発見」

European Enlightenment 「(18 世紀の) ヨーロッパで起こった啓蒙運動」

23 encapsulate 「〜を要約する」

Synthesis 「統合」

25 hallmark 「特徴」

51 1 neuroscience 「神経科学」

11 affix 「〜を押す」

21 metal smelting 「金属製錬」

25 tar 「タール」 石炭・木材を乾留して得る黒色の油状物質。

# Unit 8 "The Turk": An Ingenious Trick

**page line**

55 7 outthink 「〜より深く考える、〜の裏をかく」

56 1- Napoleon ここでは Napoleon I「ナポレオン I 世 (1769–1821：フランス皇帝)」のことを指している。

2 automaton 「自動人形、ロボット」

5 puppeteer 「人形師」

8 wonder 「驚嘆すべきもの」

16- much less teaching them to make decisions on their own 「自分で決断を下すように教えることはおろか」

20- the chess moves the automaton appeared to be making on its own 「自動人形が自分自身で行っていたと思われていたチェスの駒の動き」

28- Wolfgang von Kempelen 「ウォルフガング・フォン・ケンペレン (1734–1804)」 ハンガリーの著述家ならびに発明家。「トルコ人」というチェスを指す自動人形の発明によって有名になった。

30 cog 「(歯車の) 歯」

57 3 churn 「激しく回転する」

5 authenticity 「信頼できること、信頼性」

7 peer 「じっと見る、凝視する」

10 **wound** wind「〜のねじをまく」の過去形。

11 **whirr** 「(ウィーンと、ブンブン) 回る」

**dummy** ここでは automaton のことを指している。

21 **wow** 「(聴衆・観衆など) をやんやと言わせる、うならせる」

**populace** 「大衆、民衆、庶民」

22 **erode** 「(権威・権利など) を侵す、むしばむ」

23 **stature** 「名声、威信」

24- **it was not too much of a stretch** ここでは stretch が「無理なこと」の意味で使われており、全体では「それほど無理なことではなかった」くらいの意味になる。

58 3 **Mary Shelley** 「メアリー・シェリー (1797–1851)」 イギリスの小説家。ゴシック小説『フランケンシュタイン』の著者。

6 **portrayal** 「描写」

7- **Victor Frankenstein** 「ヴィクター・フランケンシュタイン」 イギリスの作家メアリー・シェリー作 (1818) の同名の怪奇小説の主人公。同名の主人公は自分の造った怪物のために破滅した。

10 **inanimate** 「生命のない」

18 **awe** 「(人) を畏れさせる」

**prowess** 「際立って優れた能力」

19 **envision** 「(未来のこと) を想像する、心に描く」

21 **supremacy** 「主権、優位、優勢」

# Unit 9 The "Luddites": What Were They Fighting Against?

**page line**

61 2 **Luddite** 「ラッダイト」 産業革命の 1811–17 年頃、機械が失業の原因だと誤信して機械破壊の暴動を起こした労働者。

3 **derisive** 「嘲笑的な」

5 **tech** 「工科大学、実業専門学校」

9 **Not to mention fighting a lost cause** 「成功する見込みのない運動を戦っているのは言うまでもない」

62 10 **rebel** 「反対する、反抗する」

11 **encroachment** 「侵害、侵略」

13 **livelihood** 「生計を立てていく手段」

16 **weaver** 「織工<sub>しょっこう</sub>」

18 **in a fit of rage** 「かっとなって」

21 **dispute** 「口論、けんか」

24 **vandalize** 「〜を破壊する」

29- **Outraged** 「憤慨して」

63 1 **in such a stern way** 「そのような厳格なやり方で」

| | | | |
|---|---|---|---|
| | 1- | take up the cause of ~ | 「~の主義を支持する」 |
| | 3 | mob | 「暴徒」 |
| | | storm | 「~を急襲する」 |
| | 4 | ire | 「怒り、憤り」 |
| | 5 | stocking frame | 「靴下編み機」 |
| | 6 | monstrous | 「恐るべき、とんでもない」 |
| | 7 | outproduce | 「生産力で~にまさる」 |
| | 17 | clash | 「戦闘」 |
| | 18 | horrific | 「恐ろしい、ぞっとするような」 |
| | 21 | contain | 「~を阻止する、~を食い止める」 |
| | 25 | chisel | 「のみ」 |
| | | tongs | 「ものをつまむ道具、トング」 |
| | 26 | substandard | 「標準以下の」 |
| | | masterful | 「見事な、巧みな」 |
| 64 | 4 | marvel | 「驚嘆すべきもの」 |
| | 21 | as the saying goes | 「ことわざに言うように」 |

# Unit 10  Energy: Why the 20th Century Stands Out

**page line**

| | | | |
|---|---|---|---|
| 68 | 3 | was brought to life | 「生き返った」 |
| | | lightning bolt | 「稲妻」 |
| | 5- | lay the groundwork | 「基礎・土台を作る」 |
| 69 | 8 | blubber | 「クジラ(など)の脂肪」 |
| | 11 | christen | (キリスト教徒になり洗礼名を付けることから)「~に名を付ける」 |
| | 13 | slaughter | 「(動物)を畜殺する」 |
| | 20 | all but ~ | 「ほとんど~」 |
| | 25 | fossil fuel | 「化石燃料」 |
| | 30 | hearth | 「炉床」 |
| | 30- | mine the ground for coal | 「石炭を得るために地面を掘る」 |
| 70 | 5 | Thomas Newcomen | 「トーマス・ニューコメン(1663–1729)」 イギリスの発明家。 |
| | 8 | in place | 「準備ができて、(方式・方法などが)利用されて」 |
| | 13 | James Watt | 「ジェームズ・ワット(1736–1819)」 蒸気機関を改良したスコットランドの技術者。 |
| | 24 | churn out ~ | 「(作品など)を大量に(機械的に)作り出す」 |
| | 25 | giving birth to ~ | (分詞構文で)「(その結果、現代の印刷業)を生みだした」 |
| | 29 | aqueduct | 「水路」 |
| 71 | 3- | As ingenious as the new inventions were | 「新しく発明されたものは巧妙なものであったけれども」 |
| | 10 | supercharge | 「(エンジンなど)に過給する」 |

# Unit 11　The Automobile: Bridging Two Ages

page line

# Unit 12  How Mass Media Shaped Our Ideas About AI

**page line**

81　1　**projection**「予測、予想」

　　4　**late**「最近亡くなった、故」

　　4-　**Stephen Hawking**「スティーヴン・ホーキング（1942–2018）」イギリスの物理学者。

　　5　**Elon Musk**「イーロン・マスク（1971–）」アメリカの実業家、エンジニアでスペース X 社の共同設立者および CEO。

82　1　**tune out ~**「（助言など）を無視する」

　　5　**myth**「（根拠の薄い）社会的通念、神話」

　　6　**compelling**「強い、逆らえない」

　　9　**non-divine**「神でない」

　　12　**transference**「移ること、転移」

　　23　**brew**「（混乱・波乱など）を起こす」

　　24　**disquiet**「不安、心配」

83　2　**Thomas Edison**「トーマス・エジソン（1847–1931）」アメリカの発明家。
　　　**Guglielmo Marconi**「グリエルモ・マルコーニ（1874–1937）」無線で電信を完成したイタリアの技師。

　　8　**otherworldly**「現実離れした」

　　10-　**Enrico Caruso**「エンリコ・カルーゾ（1873–1921）」イタリアのテノール。ベルカントの典型といわれる唱法で一世を風靡した。

　　14　**phonograph**「蓄音機」

　　24　**chamber**「部屋」

　　26　**Rudolph Valentino**「ルドルフ・ヴァレンティノ（1895–1926）」イタリア生まれのアメリカの映画俳優。
　　　**Lillian Gish**「リリアン・ギッシュ（1896–1993）」アメリカの無声映画俳優。
　　　**Charlie Chaplin**「チャールズ・チャップリン（1889–1977）」イギリス生まれの映画俳優・製作者。

84　4　**devour**「～をむさぼり読む、～を夢中になって見る」
　　　**subconsciously**「潜在意識的に」

　　8　**Georges Méliès**「ジョルジュ・メリエス（1861–1938）」フランスの映画監督。映画製作のパイオニア。
　　　***A Trip to the Moon***「『月世界旅行』」フランス映画（1902）。ジョルジュ・メリエス制作・脚本・監督作品。30 のシーンからなる。
　　　**sci-fi**「サイエンスフィクション」

　　10　**villain**「悪役、敵役」

　　11　**Fritz Lang**「フリッツ・ラング（1890–1976）」オーストリア生まれのアメリカの映画監督。

　　12　***Metropolis***「『メトロポリス』」ドイツ映画（1927）。フリッツ・ラング監督の作品で、西暦 2000 年における架空都市メトロポリスを舞台に、労資協調のテーマを展開した。

13 ***Star Wars*** 「『スター・ウォーズ』」 アメリカ映画（1977）。ジョージ・ルーカス脚本・監督作品。暴虐な銀河帝国の支配に対する反乱を背景として主人公ルーク・スカイウォーカーが悪と戦うスペースオペラで、西部劇・海賊映画・戦争映画などの活劇の集大成といった趣きがある。

15 **Stanley Kubrick** 「スタンリー・キューブリック（1928–99）」 アメリカの映画監督。

15- ***2001: A Space Odyssey*** 「『2001 年宇宙の旅』」 アメリカ映画（1968）。スタンリー・キューブリック監督の作品で、地球外の高等知性との接触によって人類が進化してゆくさまを描いた SF 映画。

18 **droid** 「ロボット」

19- **overlord** 「大君主、権力者」

20 ***The Terminator*** 「『ターミネーター』」 アメリカ映画（1984）。ジェームズ・キャメロン脚本(共同)・監督作品。未来社会で機械に反逆を企てる人間側のリーダー、ジョン・コナーをなきものにするため、彼が生まれる前にその母親を殺してしまうべく 2029 年の未来から 1984 年のロサンゼルスへ送り込まれた殺人アンドロイド、ターミネーター（アーノルド・シュワルツェネッガー）と人間との凄絶な戦いを描いたバイオレンスアクション。
***The Matrix*** 「『マトリックス』」 アメリカ映画（1999）。

23 **proliferate** 「急増する、激増する」

25- **mythologize** 「神話にする、神話化する」

# Unit 13　The Computer: Moonshots and Desktops

**page line**

90　1 **Charles Babbage** 「チャールズ・バベッジ（1791–1871）」 イギリスの数学者・機械工学者。近代的自動計算機械の概念の創始者。

1- **matched his chess skills against "The Turk"** 「自分のチェスの技術を（人形の）トルコ人と競わせた」

5 **prowess** 「際立って優れた腕前（能力）」

7 **hoax** 「いたずら、悪ふざけ」

9 **expose** 「〜を暴露する、〜をあばく」

91　6 **Ada Lovelace** 「エイダ・ラブレース（1815–1852）」 イギリスの数学者で、コンピュータープログラムを初めて書いた。

8 **Analytical Engine** 「解析機関」 イギリス人数学者チャールズ・バベッジが設計した、蒸気機関で動くはずだった機械式汎用コンピューター。

10 **programmability** programmable「プログラムに作ることができる」の名詞形。

18 **copious** 「多量の」

21 **Difference Engine** 「階差機関」 歴史上の機械式用途固定計算機で、多項式の数表を作成するように設計された。
**instrumental** 「助けになる」

25　**ENIAC**「エニアック」1946年にペンシルベニア大学で完成された世界最初の汎用電子計算機。

30　**aftermath**「（特に事故・災害などの）あとの状態、直後の時期、余波」

92　1　**hydrogen bomb**「水素爆弾」第二次世界大戦後、米ソ両国が冷戦下で数多くの実験を実施し、開発競争を繰り広げた。

6　**tactical**「戦術上の、戦術的な」

9　**supremacy**「主権、覇権」

10　**superpower**「（軍事力・政治力を持つ）超大国」この場合は、アメリカとソ連を指す。

20　**orbit**「軌道」

21　*Sputnik*「スプートニク」旧ソ連の人工衛星。第1号（1957年）は人類初の衛星となった。

23　**garner**「〜を（努力して）獲得する」

26　*Apollo*「アポロ」アメリカの月探査用有人宇宙船。1969年のアポロ11号が初の月面着陸。

30　**ARPANET**「アーパネット」インターネットの母体となったアメリカのコンピューター・ネットワーク。

93　21　**Steve Jobs**「スティーヴ・ジョブズ（1955–2011）」アメリカの実業家。アップル社の共同設立者の一人。

**Bill Gates**「ビル・ゲイツ（1955–）」アメリカの実業家。マイクロソフト社を設立（1975）。

# Unit 14　Data: Big, Bigger, Biggest

**page line**

98　7　**coin**「（新語など）を造り出す」

11　**in reserve**「取っておいた、蓄えてある」

12-　**should a harvest fail**「もし万一収穫高が減ってしまった場合」if a harvest should fail の if が省略され、助動詞の should が先頭に来た形。

20　**explode**「急増する、爆発的に増加する」

23　**Big Data**「ビッグデータ」通常のデータベース管理ツールでは扱えないほど膨大なデータの集まり。インターネット上のデータのほか、行政・商業データ、実験・観測により収集されるデータなどがある。

30　**warfare**「戦闘」

99　10-　**census**「人口調査、国勢調査」

16　**methodology**「方法論、方式」

19　**strategic**「戦略的な」

21　**questionnaire**「アンケート、質問表」

27　**ubiquity**「至る所に存在すること、偏在」

# Unit 15  How Far Will AI Take Us?

**page line**

103　8　**certain**「確かで、確実で」 AI's impact is certain to be huge は「AI の影響が途方もなく大きいものになるのは確実である」という意味だが、It is certain that AI's impact will be huge. と書き換えられる。

　　　**as yet**「今のところはまだ」

　　　**unanticipated**「予期しない、思いがけない」

104　1　**fall for ~**「～を信じ込む、～にだまされる」

　　2　**exponential**「（変化などが）急激な、指数的な」

　　3　**fulfill**「（希望・予言など）を実現する、遂げる」

　　4　**longing**「熱望、あこがれ」

　　5-　**Ray Kurzweil**「レイ・カーツワイル（1948-）」 アメリカの発明家、実業家で人工知能研究の世界的権威であり、特に技術的特異点（technological singularity）に関する著述で知られる。

　　15　**disrupt**「（構造）を壊す、混乱させる」

　　23-　**Universal Basic Income (UBI) distribution system**　最低限所得保障の一種で、政府がすべての国民に対して最低限の生活を送るのに必要とされている額の現金を定期的に支給するというシステム。

105　10　**beloved**「かわいい、いとしい」

　　15　**R2D2**「アールツーディーツー」 アメリカの SF 映画『スター・ウォーズ』シリーズに登場するキャラクター。

　　20　**inevitable**「避けられない、必然的な」

　　28-　**analytical**「分析的な、分析的思考にたけた」

106　17　**optimum**「最適の」

　　17-　**peak-efficiency distribution and transportation channels**「最高に効率的な流通と輸送経路」

　　25　**arc**「（物語などの）展開、進展」

# Photo Credits

## Unit 1
**p.10** ©Smrm1977 (null) | Dreamstime.com
©Iakov Filimonov | Dreamstime.com
**p.12** ©Kittipong Jirasukhanont | Dreamstime.com

## Unit 2
**p.16** ©Joanne Zhe | Dreamstime.com
**p.17** ©Neil Harrison | Dreamstime.com
**p.19** ©Cobalt88 | Dreamstime.com

## Unit 3
**p.22** ©Andrii Yalanskyi | Dreamstime.com
**p.23** ©Department of Energy, Office of Public Affairs
**p.25** ©Airphoto | Dreamstime.com

## Unit 4
**p.28** ©Scaliger | Dreamstime.com
**p.29** ©Demerzel21 | Dreamstime.com
**p.30** ©Sorin Colac | Dreamstime.com
**p.31** ©RightFramePhotoVideo | Dreamstime.com

## Unit 5
**p.35** ©Eleftherios Damianidis | Dreamstime.com
**p.36** ©Tupungato | Dreamstime.com
**p.37** ©Cosmin Danila | Dreamstime.com
**p.38** ©Bedardar | Dreamstime.com

## Unit 6
**p.42** ©Oleg Zaikin | Dreamstime.com
**p.43** ©Travis Rogers | Dreamstime.com
**p.44** ©Gérard Janot

## Unit 7
**p.48** ©Thomas Lammeyer | Dreamstime.com
**p.49** ©Linda Williams | Dreamstime.com
**p.50** ©Mawerix | Dreamstime.com
**p.51** ©dronepicr

## Unit 8
**p.55** Public Domain

**p.56** Public Domain
**p.58** Public Domain
Public Domain

**Unit 9**
**p.61** Public Domain
**p.62** Public Domain
**p.63** ©Rene Drouyer | Dreamstime.com

**Unit 10**
**p.68** Public Domain
**p.69** ©Daniel Logan | Dreamstime.com
**p.70** ©Simonhs | Dreamstime.com
**p.71** ©Marcovarro | Dreamstime.com
Public Domain

**Unit 11**
**p.75** ©Raytags | Dreamstime.com
**p.76** Public Domain
**p.77** Public Domain

**Unit 12**
**p.81** ©Marotistock | Dreamstime.com
**p.82** Public Domain
**p.83** Public Domain

**Unit 13**
**p.90** Public Domain
**p.91** ©Massimo Parisi | Dreamstime.com
**p.92** Public Domain
**p.93** ©Featureflash | Dreamstime.com
©St3fano | Dreamstime.com

**Unit 14**
**p.97** ©Valeriya Potapova | Dreamstime.com
**p.98** ©Pressmaster | Dreamstime.com
**p.100** ©Mariia Boiko | Dreamstime.com

**Unit 15**
**p.103** ©Andrey Armyagov | Dreamstime.com
**p.105** ©Dmytro Zinkevych | Dreamstime.com
**p.106** ©Tero Vesalainen | Dreamstime.com

本書には音声CD（別売）があります

# The Road to AI
## Mankind's Technological Journey
AIへの道―テクノロジーと人類の進歩

2021年 1 月20日　初版第 1 刷発行
2024年 2 月20日　初版第 5 刷発行

著　者　Andy　Boerger

編注者　花　﨑　一　夫
　　　　花　﨑　美　紀

発行者　福　岡　正　人

発行所　　株式会社　金星堂

（〒101-0051）東京都千代田区神田神保町 3-21
Tel. (03) 3263-3828（営業部）
(03) 3263-3997（編集部）
Fax (03) 3263-0716
https://www.kinsei-do.co.jp

編集担当　池田恭子　　　　　　　　　Printed in Japan
印刷所／日新印刷株式会社　製本所／松島製本
ISBN978-4-7647-4124-9　C1082